WHAT HAPPENS
WHEN STUDENTS
OWN THEIR LEARNING

EMPOWER

JOHN SPENCER AND A.J. JULIANI

This book is available at special discounts when purchased in quantity for use as premiums, promotions, fundraisers, or for educational use. For inquiries and details, contact the publisher at books@impressbooks.org.

Published by IMPRESS,
a division of Dave Burgess Consulting, Inc.
ImpressBooks.org
daveburgessconsulting.com

Library of Congress Control Number: 2017944259
Paperback ISBN: 978-1-946444-43-1
eBook ISBN: 978-1-946444-42-4

First Printing: June 2017

CONTENTS

FOREWORD
BY GEORGE COUROS

Recently I was listening to a teacher talk about their more "traditional" view of education and how "compliance" wasn't a bad thing for students. He even went a step further, saying students should be "obedient."

I cringed a little.

Okay, maybe a lot.

First off, let's look at the definition of *obedient*:

Obedient—complying or willing to comply with orders or requests; submissive to another's will.

Is this what we really want from our students? That they are simply submissive to the will of their teachers? Do we want to develop generations of students that will challenge conventional ideas and think for themselves—or simply do what they are told?

I do not know many teachers who would want to be "obedient" to their principals. We teach the "golden rule" to our students; we must follow it ourselves.

So let's look at the word *compliant*.

Compliant—inclined to agree with others or obey rules, especially to an excessive degree; acquiescent.

Is compliance a bad thing to teach in education? Not really. In some ways, people have to be compliant. Think of tax season. You have to be compliant with the rules that are set out by your government.

As educators, there are times when we have to be compliant in our work as well. You have deadlines that you have to meet (i.e., report cards).

Compliance is not a bad word, but it should not be our end goal in education. My belief is that we need to move beyond compliance, past engagement, and on to empowerment.

These ideas are not separate but, in some ways, can be seen as a continuum.

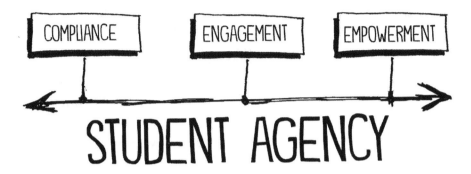

Let's go back to the word *compliance*. Has that really ever been the end goal of schools? Maybe as a system overall, but I think the best educators have always tried to empower their students. They know that if you are truly good at your job as an educator, eventually the students will not need you.

That is why "lifelong learning" has been a goal in education forever. If our students are truly compliant when they walk out of schools, they will always need someone else's rules to follow. To develop the "leaders of tomorrow," we need to develop them as leaders today.

Focusing on empowering students is seen by some as "fluffy;" students just show up to school to do whatever they want. This is not my belief at all.

Empowering students teaches them to have their own voice and follow their own direction, but if they are going to be successful, they will need to truly have the discipline (using the definition, "train oneself to do something in a controlled and habitual way") to make it happen. "Empowerment" and "hard work" are not mutually exclusive; in fact, both elements are needed to make a true difference in our world.

Think about how many of our kids in school talk about becoming "YouTubers." If you truly want to make that happen, you do not apply to some job, but you *will* have to focus on creating content consistently over time while building an audience. This might be your dream, but to make it happen, there is a lot of work to be done. Becoming a content creator allows you to follow your own path, yet to be successful, hard work is needed.

I love this quote:[1]

"HARD WORK DOES NOT GUARANTEE SUCCESS, BUT LACK OF HARD WORK GUARANTEES THAT THERE WILL BE NO SUCCESS."

—JIMMY V

Helping students find their own paths—not the ones we set out for them—has always been the focus in education, yet we need to be more explicit about this path.

A.J. Juliani and John Spencer do a great job of sharing why empowering our students is not only important in our world today but crucial. As they state, this is about shifting our mindset, which will ultimately lead to students not only *believing* they can change the world, but *doing it* because of school.

We all want our students to be respectful to educators and peers. Hopefully, we all want them to walk out of school, become intrinsically motivated, and find their own ways to success and happiness. Compliance is sometimes a part of this, but it is not the end goal. Are we trying to develop students to fit into our world, or are we hoping students feel they have the power to create a better world both now and in the future?[2]

"THE PEOPLE WHO ARE CRAZY ENOUGH TO THINK THEY CAN CHANGE THE WORLD ARE THE ONES WHO DO."
—STEVE JOBS

Your legacy as an educator is always determined by what your students do. You change the world by empowering your students to do the same.

FINDING
YOUR
VOICE

She came rushing up to me in a panic at the start of class.

"What's wrong, Katie? Everything okay?"

"Well, Mr. J, I'm going to have to change my project. I really like making my own pair of sandals, but I just have to change what I'm doing. Is that allowed? Will I lose points for switching my project?"

We were in the middle of our first attempt at a 20% Time project in my class. My students were given 20 percent of their time to work on something about which they were passionate and curious, and they had to take their learning and make something for a final project.

Katie had been quiet for most of the project. She didn't get fired up like a lot of my students when it was first introduced. She didn't ask a lot of questions about how it would be graded or why we were doing something different.

In fact, she had enjoyed her time so far, making sandals. It was a project that meant something to her, so I was surprised to see how anxious she was to change her project.

I responded, "Yes, you can change your project, but I thought you liked what you were doing."

Katie explained that she wanted to learn sign language. Her young cousin was deaf, and she had always told herself she would learn sign language when she had time.

But between school, sports, and a summer packed with work she kept on putting it off.

Now her cousin was coming to live with her family for a short period of time due to a house fire. The situation was awful. It was even more heartbreaking to Katie because she had never taken the time to learn sign language.

The 20% Time project had given her a new hope that she might have some time to learn sign language in school.

Our conversation ended with me saying, "This is why we are doing this project. I want you to be able to learn because you have a purpose for learning beyond a grade. I'm going to help you learn sign language as best I can in the next six weeks!"

But I didn't know a thing about sign language.

IN FACT, I DIDN'T KNOW A THING ABOUT MOST OF THE PROJECTS ON WHICH MY STUDENTS WERE WORKING.

Sure, they were reading, writing, speaking, listening, and creating. But it was one of the first moments I ever felt helpless as a teacher, because I was not the content expert in the classroom on what my students were learning.

Yet I had a number of students like Katie (engaged and excited to learn), so I pushed forward. I helped her research local groups that used sign language; she jumped on YouTube Channels teaching her how to start learning sign language and even Skyped with one of the people who started this YouTube channel.

She was learning, but she was also making. She was solving her own problems and coming up with ways to learn faster and share that learning with the world on her blog.

When it came time for our class to present in TED-style talks, I wasn't exactly sure what Katie had planned for her presentation.

That day, as I was rushing around to make sure everything was working, I missed seeing her Aunt and cousin walk into the auditorium and greet Katie.

After a few of her classmates had already presented, she stepped on stage to share her learning journey.

Katie was shy, and she was shaky at first in front of the audience. As she shared why she changed her project, the crowd began to engage in her story. At the end of her talk she told us that she had been working on learning the words to the song, "I Hope You Dance," and was going to perform it in sign language.

People began to tear up immediately as the song started over the speakers, and she began to sign.

I found myself mesmerized by this shy young woman expressing such emotion and grace on stage. It is something I'll never forget.

Just then, in the midst of this wonderful moment, the technology stopped working. The sound cut off, and the crowd began to murmur and look around in surprise.

I scrambled for what felt like five minutes (but was really only five seconds), trying to fix the problem. Underneath a table, looking for an aux cord, I heard the audience whispering completely stop.

Katie had started to sing the song herself, *acapella*. She was signing and singing at the same time, continuing right where the music left off.

It was beautiful.

Tears came to my eyes, and as she finished, the audience erupted into a standing ovation. Katie, a bit red in the face, gave a quick wave good-bye and rushed off the stage.

The next day in class, we had a round table reflection on the project and final presentations. Every student wanted to know how Katie had pulled this off. They wanted to know how she kept singing when the music stopped. What she said next will always stay with me:

"I didn't want to let my cousin down. And I didn't want to let all the people who helped me learn sign language down. I think though, what really got me is that I didn't want to let myself down. I'd never worked so hard on a school assignment before. I spent hours and hours after school and on the weekends to get prepared. If I had stopped, that work may have been for nothing. Really, I didn't even give myself an option not to continue and finish the song in some way."

This story changed the way I thought about student work. For years, I had worked so hard to inspire, challenge, and engage my students.

Now the tables had turned.

Katie inspired me. She inspired her classmates. She inspired that audience, and her story continues to inspire today.

Yet this was one student. I wish I could say every student of mine had at least one experience in school like this.

Most did not.

I was never a perfect teacher. Not all of my students were empowered like Katie was in this project. And I didn't spend 100 percent of my time embracing this type of empowered learning that was happening in my classroom that day.

But it was a start.

After this project, I shifted my focus. It wasn't easy. It was extremely messy. But it was worth it. Empowering students became my goal, and giving students the opportunity to pursue their passions, goals, and future was the mission.

THE NUMBERS ARE
STAGGERING

583 DAYS

FOURTEEN THOUSAND HOURS

840,000 MINUTES

If you grew up in the United States or a country with similar education structure, chances are you spent 6.64 hours per day in school, 180 days a year, for 12–13 years.[3]

THAT'S OVER FOURTEEN THOUSAND HOURS (OR 840,000 MINUTES), NO MATTER HOW YOU SLICE IT.

The 6.64 average hours a day in school is actually better represented in minutes.

400 MINUTES PER DAY

What are we doing with all of this time? More importantly, what are our students doing?

We aren't asking what are our students are learning during the fourteen thousand hours they spend in school. That is already well documented.

Everyone knows you learn your basic reading, writing, and math skills in the younger grades, and then start to get very specific with world history classes, physics and biology classes, and algebra and geometry classes as we get older.

We've been learning the same subjects in the same pattern for quite some time. Are there variations of this?

Sure.

Are we going to assume most of you reading this book are following the traditional education path laid out more than one hundred years ago?

Yes.

The question is, what are our students **doing** during these classes?

Are they taking notes? Are they listening to adults speak? Are they studying for tests and quizzes? Are they watching PowerPoint slides move across the screen? Are they filling out worksheets and packets? Are they regurgitating information, filling out problems, and checking their answers in the back of the textbook? Are they writing research papers? Are they raising their hands? Are they sitting in the chairs for 80 percent of the day?

Are they following procedures, filling in bubbles, watching the clock, and acting appropriately compliant in every way possible so as not to upset the adults in charge?

Or are they building the knowledge and the skills to pursue *their* passions, interests, and future?

WHAT ARE THEY DOING?

If you grew up in an education setting like we did, then you spent much of your time being actively compliant—trying to navigate a system that was designed to produce people who followed the rules and waited to be told what to do. Then you graduated. And you waited for someone to tell you what to do.

It was a dependable formula. You went to school, followed the rules, graduated, and stepped into a job as a compliant worker.

THE OLD FORMULA

GO TO SCHOOL   FOLLOW   GRADUATE   BE A COMPLIANT
                  THE RULES   WORKER

HOWEVER, TIMES HAVE CHANGED.

OUR WORLD WANTS
GO-GETTERS.

IT WANTS
DECISION MAKERS.

IT WANTS
DESIGNERS, CREATORS,
AND DREAMERS.

As author and *New York Times'* columnist Thomas Friedman aptly points out,[4]

"THE WORLD ONLY CARES ABOUT—AND PAYS OFF ON—WHAT YOU CAN DO WITH WHAT YOU KNOW (AND IT DOESN'T CARE HOW YOU LEARNED IT)."

So why do we spend so much time in school, playing the game of school, following rules, and waiting for others to tell us what to do? Why do we rarely give students choice in what they learn, how they learn, when they learn, and why they learn?

This problem extends well beyond school. It impacts us as adults. Those fourteen thousand hours we spent in school from K–12 really do make a difference in how we see the world.

Have you ever met an adult who doesn't really love what they do, who is just going through the motions in their job and everyday life? Even sadder, how many people have you talked with who constantly complain, showing no visible passion for anything in the world?

I'm sure that, like me, you have met those people. I've also seen the making of these adults in schools across our country: students who are consistently being "prepared" for the next test, assessment, or grade level ... only to find out after graduation that they don't really know what their passions really are.

They feel lost and confused.

These are the same students who are never allowed to learn what they want in school. Forced down a curriculum path that we believe is "best for them," they discover it is a path that offers very little choice in subject matter and learning outcomes.

It would be too easy to throw up our hands and blame "the system" or "the politicians" or anyone else for the game of school that students are playing.

It's also pretty easy to say that we went through the same system, and we turned out fine!

BUT WE WOULD BE MISSING THE POINT.

School doesn't have to look like this, because the world and natural learning doesn't look like this.

But what can you do? It's not as easy as inventing a new school or designing a new curriculum. You have a test, a curriculum map, a bell schedule, and a set of programs that often push compliance over empowerment.

But you are still the one who can transform the learning space. You are the one to innovate. You are the one who spends hours with your students.

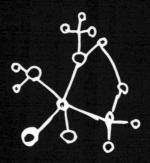

WE DON'T HAVE TO CHANGE THE ENTIRE SYSTEM IN ORDER TO GIVE OUR STUDENTS A DIFFERENT EXPERIENCE.

INSTEAD, WE ONLY NEED TO CHANGE ONE THING:

We need to shift our mindset from compliance (students must follow our rules) and engagement (getting kids excited about our chosen content, curriculum, and activities) to empowerment.

As former Teacher of the Year (still currently teaching) and author Bill Ferriter describes[5] so clearly,

"EMPOWERING STUDENTS MEANS GIVING KIDS THE KNOWLEDGE AND SKILLS TO PURSUE *THEIR* PASSIONS, INTERESTS, AND FUTURE."

—BILL FERRITER

When we empower students, the fourteen thousand hours have a new purpose. It's not all about what we want students to learn, it is about what they learn through their choices in what they do (create, build, design, make, evaluate).

This book is about that shift.

Most teachers would agree wholeheartedly that our students need to be more engaged. They'd raise their hands in unanimous affirmation if asked, "Would you like your students to be more engaged in class?"

As teachers, we say the same thing.

Engagement is more powerful than compliance.

Phil Schlechty, who founded the Center for Engagement, describes engagement as the merging of two key factors: high attention and high commitment.[6]

When students have high attention, they are focused on the learning and what they are doing.

When students have high commitment, it means they'll push through the ups and downs of learning something new and challenging.

SCHLECTY'S LEVELS OF ENGAGEMENT

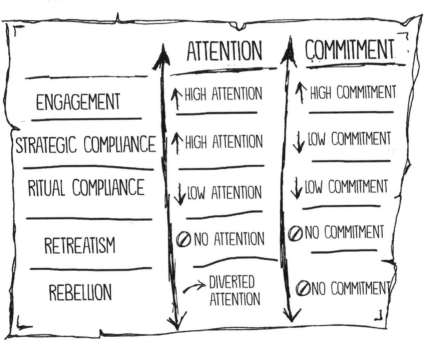

	ATTENTION	COMMITMENT
ENGAGEMENT	↑ HIGH ATTENTION	↑ HIGH COMMITMENT
STRATEGIC COMPLIANCE	↑ HIGH ATTENTION	↓ LOW COMMITMENT
RITUAL COMPLIANCE	↓ LOW ATTENTION	↓ LOW COMMITMENT
RETREATISM	⊘ NO ATTENTION	⊘ NO COMMITMENT
REBELLION	→ DIVERTED ATTENTION	⊘ NO COMMITMENT

Still, engagement is only half the battle.

When students are engaged, they are attentive to our chosen content and objectives. They are giving their full focus to the resources, texts, and problems we are asking them to solve. They are being committed to completing our curriculum and assessments in ways in which we have asked them to demonstrate mastery.

What about the problems they want to solve? The topics they find interesting? The areas they want to dive deeper into and learn more about?

What about their future? The one where they will have to make their own paths, decide what challenges to tackle, and what opportunities to take. The future where they will struggle, make mistakes, and not be sure what direction is best.

Our goals have to change.

LAYING THE GROUNDWORK

This book lays the groundwork for making this shift. When we shift from preparing students for what's next, to helping them prepare for anything, a world of possibilities open up in their learning.

OUR JOB IS NOT TO PREPARE STUDENTS FOR SOMETHING; OUR JOB IS TO HELP STUDENTS PREPARE THEMSELVES FOR ANYTHING.

HOW WE MAKE THE SHIFT AS TEACHERS AND LEADERS

ENGAGEMENT → EMPOWERMENT

ENGAGED ENVIRONMENTS	EMPOWERED ENVIRONMENTS
ATTENTIVE AND COMMITTED TO OUR CURRICULUM	ATTENTIVE AND COMMITTED TO THEIR INTERESTS
"PREPARING FOR THEIR FUTURE JOBS"	"PREPARING THEMSELVES FOR ANYTHING"
TEACHERS WORKING TO "MAKE IT INTERESTING"	TEACHERS WORKING ON "TAPPING INTO THEIR INTERESTS"
YOU MUST LEARN _____	WHAT DO YOU WANT TO LEARN?
GIVING CHOICE	INSPIRING POSSIBILITIES
FOLLOWING THE BEATEN PATH	MAKING YOUR OWN PATH
TAKING AN ASSESSMENT	ASSESSING YOUR OWN LEARNING
CONSUMING	CREATING
DIFFERENTIATED INSTRUCTION	PERSONALIZED LEARNING

You may be reading this and nodding your head, thinking, "YES!" At the same time you may also have lots of questions. Don't worry, this is completely natural. We've asked these same questions ourselves plenty of times:

WHAT ABOUT CLASSROOM MANAGEMENT?

WHAT ABOUT THE CURRICULUM MAP?

WHAT ABOUT THE TESTS?

WHAT ABOUT THE STRUCTURE OF SCHOOL?

Here's the thing: We aren't going to argue about all the things we'd like to change about school but don't have control over.

Instead, we are going to focus on the areas we have control and influence over as teachers, instructional coaches, or school leaders.

Will your students still have to take some tests? **Most likely.**

Will your students still have a curriculum pre-designed for them? **Most likely.**

Will your students' learning look messy? **Most definitely.**

Will school still have bells and follow a similar structure? **All signs point to yes.**

But that doesn't mean we stop. It means we take the large majority of those fourteen thousand hours that we have some influence over and **use them to inspire creativity and innovation** in our learners.

If classroom management is an issue, give students choice in what they learn, and watch their focus increase on learning what interests them, even if it is a challenging topic.

Teach above the test. Have students learn beyond the test. When students are making, designing, creating, and evaluating, they are going way past what tests cover.

Would you rather have a disengaged, compliance-driven student take a test, or an empowered maker and designer take the test?

Curriculum and standards will always play a role. But standards should not hold you back from creating an empowering learning environment.

Standards are the architect's blueprint, and you, the teacher, are still the builder and designer. When you include students in the learning design process, the possibilities are endless of what the architect's blueprint will actually look like in real life.

Instead of worrying about how the school year and school day is structured, absorb the concepts of this book. It will help you develop ways to build an empowered environment in the structures you set up as a teacher.

IN OTHER WORDS, THIS BOOK IS ABOUT SOLUTIONS.

Throughout this book, we'll tackle each of these issues head-on and find actionable ways you can overcome the tests, curriculum, and classroom management issues to create an empowered experience for every student.

WHAT THIS BOOK IS	WHAT THIS BOOK ISN'T
A BOOK OF IDEAS	AN INSTRUCTION MANUAL
REAL STORIES FROM REAL CLASSROOMS	A RESEARCH-BASED JOURNAL ARTICLE
FOCUS ON SOLUTIONS	FOCUS ON PROBLEMS
STUDENT DRIVEN	TEACHER DRIVEN
ASKS QUESTIONS	ANSWERS ALL YOUR QUESTIONS
FUN AND UPLIFTING	SERIOUS AND PROPER

FOR THE CURIOUS ONES

This book is for the curious ones asking hard questions, wondering what it might mean to move from engagement to empowerment.

This book is for the teachers with bold ideas that seem impractical and impossible to pull off. This is for the teachers waiting for permission to take the plunge into student choice. If that's you, please read this book as a challenge to take action and to chase that moonshot idea of student choice. Because nobody's going to give you permission.

Empower is for curious teachers who want something they can use right now. *Empower* is for leaders who want to help move into a learner-centered environment. *Empower* is for teachers who are willing to make the jump, even if it means stepping out of their comfort zone and trying something new.

FOR THE WILD ONES

This book is for the wild ones, the innovators, the teachers who are rewriting the rules.

This is for the teachers who refuse to teach the way they were taught just because that's how it's always been done. This is for those who are already empowering their students to own the learning.

If that's you, please read this as an affirmation of some of the great stuff you're already doing in the classroom. Read this book as a thank you note for the work you are doing.

SOME REALLY GOOD REASONS NOT TO READ THIS BOOK...

You've probably noticed that this book looks a little different than most teacher books.

So we're just going to put it out there. *Empower* isn't for everyone.

It is not for those looking for a doctoral thesis or a journal article. It's not a comprehensive, definitive textbook on student-centered learning.

It is not for those who already consider themselves experts on empowering students.

It is not for those who believe students should just behave and do what they're told.

EMPOWER IS FOR ALL OF US
WHO WANT TO SHIFT SCHOOL
TO BE LESS
ABOUT DOING
SCHOOL

AND MORE
ABOUT DOING LEARNING.

Empowered learners are the future of our world, and how they spend their fourteen thousand hours will determine not only their future but the future of generations to come.

ARE YOU READY TO JUMP INTO THIS JOURNEY OF EMPOWERING LEARNERS WITH US?

We can't wait to see what your learners do because you decided to make the shift to helping students prepare themselves for anything!

WARNING:

We don't have all the answers.

We're still asking questions.

We can't give you a magical formula. We're still experimenting.

We can't offer an app or a system or a program because real change happens from within.

The **bad news** is, there is no instruction manual.

THE GOOD NEWS IS, THERE IS NO INSTRUCTION MANUAL.

WE'RE ALL JUST MAKING IT UP AS WE GO.

SO CONSIDER THIS BOOK AN INVITATION TO JOIN US ON THIS JOURNEY FULL OF MISTAKES AND SCRAPED KNEES AND MOMENTS OF INFURIATING CONFUSION.

PRETTY GLAMOROUS, RIGHT?

TRUST US. IT'S TOTALLY WORTH IT, BECAUSE EPIC THINGS HAPPEN WHEN YOU EMPOWER YOUR STUDENTS TO OWN THEIR LEARNING.

CHAPTER 1

A SNAPSHOT OF STUDENT OWNERSHIP AND A TEACHER WHO CHANGED THE WORLD

This was me (John) in the eighth grade. If you can't see me, it's because I was invisible.

And that's how I liked it.

My entire goal was to go unnoticed. Fly under the radar. Keep away from the Cool Patrol (the people who ran the school's social hierarchy).

I had one friend, this kid named Matt. We were two nerds in a pod.

And fortunately for me, he had perfect attendance year after year.

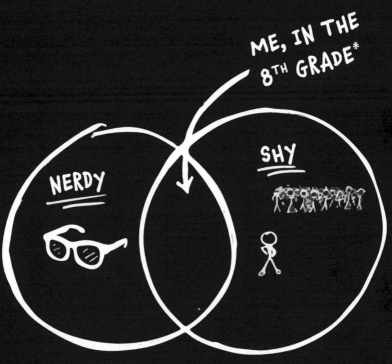

So that was my system: find one friend and hang out with him and fly under the radar.

And it worked—until one day it didn't.

One afternoon, he was gone from school. Nothing serious. He had a cold. But I remember looking out at the sea of students and thinking, *I hope one person invites me to their lunch table.*

It didn't happen.

I waited for an eternity, paralyzed by fear. Finally I tossed my food in the trash and hid out in the bathroom, which might be the grossest place in school to hide out.

But here's the thing: My plan had worked. Nobody had noticed me. And it felt horrible.

Despite all of this, I had two teachers, Mrs. Smoot and Mr. Darrow, who saw me as a person.

They knew I cared about social justice and baseball and history, so they invited me to do a History Day project.

At first it was fun (if a little overwhelming). I had to plan the entire project and track my own progress. I had to figure out what questions to ask and where to find the answers. I had to narrow down my topic to something I cared about—in this case, Jackie Robinson and the racial integration of baseball. Then it became terrifying.

I wrote letters to newscasters and made phone calls to former players. I remember picking up the phone, my hands trembling as I read aloud my pre-recorded script and waited for the stranger to respond. I eventually worked on a slide presentation. (Back in the day when you had to take pictures and go to the drug store to have them converted into little plastic slides.)

However, the most nerve-wracking moment occurred when I sat in a radio studio recording my script. I would play the giant magnetic tape back and use a razor to cut it and Scotch tape to splice it together. I listened to my voice and hated it.

At one point, I threw my hands up in the air. "I'm not doing this," I said.

But Mrs. Smoot looked me in the eyes and said,

"I'M NOT GOING TO LET YOU GET AWAY WITH THAT. WHAT YOU SAY MATTERS. AND WHEN YOU CHOOSE TO STAY SILENT, YOU ROB THE WORLD OF YOUR CREATIVITY."

Those words stuck with me forever.

I finished the project, and it continued to be terrifying. I remember the moment I presented to my classmates, and one of the members of the Cool Patrol started a slow clap. At first, I thought he was mocking me. But as others cheered, I realized something.

I wasn't invisible.

I went on to present at the state and national competition. It was a powerful experience.

And the most powerful part of it was the ownership. I had never owned my learning like that before.

That year had a lasting impact—one that continues even now. Mrs. Smoot's influence shapes how I teach and how I parent and the creative work I do on a daily basis.

I became a different person—not because of the program or even the process but because of a teacher who saw something in me that I couldn't see in myself.

That was empowering.

I became a maker.

And while I didn't recognize it at the time, that experience ultimately shaped why I became a teacher.

THE MOST
POWERFUL THING
YOU CAN DO IS
EMPOWER YOUR
STUDENTS.

THEY BECOME PROBLEM-SOLVERS

THEY CULTIVATE COOL, GEEKY INTERESTS

THEY VIEW MISTAKES AS LEARNING OPPORTUNITIES

THEY DEVELOP A GROWTH MINDSET

THEY ARE MORE CREATIVE

THEY LEARN PROJECT MANAGEMENT

WHAT HAPPENS WHEN STUDENTS OWN THEIR LEARNING?

THEY LEARN TO EXPERIMEN

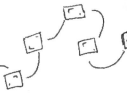

THEY DEVELOP ITERATIVE THINKING

THEY BECOME EXPLORERS

THEY ARE READY FOR THE GLOBAL CREATIVE ECONOMY

THEY LEARN TO THINK OUTSIDE THE BOX

THEY BECOME SYSTEMS THINKERS

THEY ARE SELF-DIRECTED

IN OTHER WORDS, THEY BECOME PASSIONATE, LIFELONG LEARNERS, READY TO TACKLE THE WORLD.*

* Figuratively, because literally tackling the world would be dangerous and impractical.

Visit EmpowerBook.co to get practical resources for empowering our learners. Join the discussion online using the hashtag #empowerbook.

CHAPTER 2

OUR JOB AS TEACHERS, PARENTS,
AND LEADERS IS NOT TO PREPARE
KIDS FOR "SOMETHING;"

OUR JOB IS TO HELP KIDS
PREPARE THEMSELVES
FOR "ANYTHING."

STUDENTS   ANYTHING

Louis[7] was born in 1809 in a small village just east of Paris. He was the youngest of four, and his mother and father worked the countryside making things out of leather. By all accounts, Louis had a wonderful experience growing up, even after the accident that occurred when he was only three years old.

In his father's workshop, Louis was trying to make some holes in the leather using a tool called an awl. The awl looked like a sharp-pointed screwdriver and was used to make such things as belt holes. While he was pressing it into a piece of leather, the awl slipped and caught Louis in the eye. He was rushed to be seen by surgeons, but the doctors could not save his eye, and they put a patch on it. Weeks later Louis's other eye became infected, and by the age of five he had lost all sight.

In part because of his young age, Louis did not realize that he had lost his sight. His parents said that he would ask why it was so dark, as the child seemed confused about being blind.

Louis's parents did not hold him back. He was not treated as disabled and instead learned to travel around the village and country paths with various canes his father had created for him. He continued to learn, tinker, and create despite the loss of sight. His teachers and local villagers continued to help him learn until, at the age of ten, Louis attended the Royal Institute for Blind Youth.

While there, Louis learned about a communication system called night writing, devised by Captain Charles Barbier of the French Army. The system, which was a series of complicated dots and dashes impressed into paper for communicating without light (and without sound), was extremely complex.

However, by the age of fifteen, Louis Braille had taken these ideas and developed his own system for reading and writing for the blind, aptly named the Braille System.

Louis Braille went on to be an inventor, professor, and musician who continued to fine-tune the Braille System until his passing in 1852. Still, Braille did not become widely used until years later when it was seen as a revolutionary way to adapt languages across the world.

WHY IS EMPOWERING OUR LEARNERS SO IMPORTANT?

Louis Braille is only one example of what happens when learners are encouraged and motivated to solve problems that matter to them and dive into interests that are relevant to their own lives.

There was every reason in the world for Louis to live a life devoid of creating, designing, building, and inventing. He was not from a wealthy family. He had lost his vision at a young age. He lived in a time where many saw education as a privilege and not a right.

But Louis's story can serve as a reason for us to focus on giving kids the knowledge and skills to pursue *their* passions, interests, and future.

WHAT'S THE BEST THAT COULD HAPPEN?

As we get started in making the shift, let's begin with six learning truths that are going to be the foundation for the rest of this book.

Often we focus on doing new things in new ways, without starting with a strong tree trunk of best practices and beliefs that stand the test of time. Here are our six truths that will drive the rest of this book and ultimately drive our thinking on the need for empowering our learners.

TRUTH #1

EVERY CHILD DESERVES TO OWN THEIR LEARNING. TEACHERS CAN EMPOWER STUDENT OWNERSHIP OF LIFELONG LEARNING.

Truth #1 is the reason we educate students. It's for their benefit.

But it only matters to our students when they own the learning. When we give students choice, allow for inquiry, and foster creativity, we see the amazing things they can do.

Technology plays an interesting role in student ownership. That device in their pockets has all the information in the world. It can connect them to anyone, allow for collaboration, and be used for a variety of innovative purposes.

As teachers, we have to embrace the notion that technology can open up a world of learning opportunities and then give our students the chance to own those opportunities.

TRUTH #2

EVERY CHILD IN YOUR CLASS IS SOMEONE ELSE'S WHOLE WORLD. EMPOWERING STUDENTS TRANSFORMS OUR SOCIAL/HUMAN CONNECTIONS.

Truth #2 comes from a quote I (A.J.) first heard Tom Murray say on stage: "Every child in your class is someone else's whole world."

As a parent who now has a child in school, this really hits home for me as I watch my daughter leave for school every day. Empowered learning brings us closer together through communication tools, real-time collaboration, and sharing meaningful and relevant work that brings the learning to life.

But it does more than that. It transforms our social/human connections with little moments that can make a kid's day or make a parent proud.

16

TRUTH #3

STORIES WILL ALWAYS SHAPE US. THEY WILL ALWAYS HELP US LEARN. EMPOWER STUDENTS TO CREATE AND SHARE THEIR LEARNING STORIES.

Truth #3 is all about the story.

It's one of the best ways to teach and a favorite way of ours to learn. Stories have passed the test of time, and continue to enlighten and motivate people every day to learn and grow.

Our current world has transformed storytelling. Technology expands our depth of story and allows us to share stories wider and farther than ever before. When something goes "viral," it means a story has struck a chord and reached millions of people unlike at any other time in history. As teachers and students, we can use technology to transform our storytelling and how we learn.

The true power of a story comes from two things: learning from the story and then sharing your story with an audience and with the world. Empowered learners know stories are the gateway to pursuing their passions and future.

17

TRUTH #4

THE ONLY THING YOU CAN PREPARE STUDENTS FOR IS AN UNPREDICTABLE WORLD.

Truth #4 is something I firmly believe and try to say every time I speak at a conference or school. As mentioned earlier, our job as teachers is to help students prepare themselves for anything. To frame this as a story, we are the guides, and our students are the heroes of the story.

When we don't know what the future holds for our students, our job changes. Teachers can be guides who empower learners because we can be free of always having to be the content experts (especially as content continually changes). Instead, we share with our students that we ,too, are master learners. Knowing how to learn is a skill we can share with our students to help them learn anything.

TRUTH #5

LITERACY IS ABOUT LEARNING, AND LEARNING IS ABOUT UNLEARNING AND RELEARNING.

Truth #5 is based around this quote: "The illiterate of the twenty-first century will not be those who cannot read and write, but those who cannot learn, unlearn, and relearn."[8]

Empowered students are part of a learning environment where unlearning and relearning is the norm. This type of environment is where we can get new information and analyze it, apply it, and use it to create or evaluate. Empowered learners adopt a mindset that praises unlearning and relearning and treats the process as a continuum.

TRUTH #6

AS TEACHERS, WE HAVE A HUGE IMPACT ON OUR STUDENTS' LIVES. EMPOWERING OUR STUDENTS AMPLIFIES THAT IMPACT.

Truth #6 is something all of us who work in education know: **We have an impact.** We make a difference. It's why we got into this profession in the first place, and it's what keeps us here and moving even on the hardest days.

Empowered environments allow our connections and impact to move beyond the classroom walls and continue to be powerful, long after our students are out of sight.

There is no better time to be in education than right now. Education is the bridge to so many opportunities for our learners. We must step aside as the gatekeepers and instead move next to our learners to take the journey together.

These six truths help us to stand firm against the fads and next "best thing" in education while focusing on what works to make our learners' experience both meaningful and relevant while they are in school.

Visit EmpowerBook.co to get practical resources for empowering our learners. Join the discussion online using the hashtag #empowerbook.

CHAPTER 3

EMPOWERING STUDENTS MEANS
GIVING KIDS THE KNOWLEDGE AND
SKILLS TO PURSUE THEIR PASSIONS,
INTERESTS, AND FUTURE.

SKILLS   PURSUE THEIR PASSIONS

THE SHIFT FROM
"MAKING THE SUBJECT INTERESTING"

TO TAPPING INTO
STUDENT INTERESTS

When I was in high school, I (A.J.) spent most of my time playing sports (football and basketball) and worrying about my so-called social life. I rarely was allowed to explore my interests in school and thus set up a mental block against caring about anything academic. Even when we would do something fun or exciting in class, I would never fully allow myself to embrace the activity or follow up on my own time.

In that pre-Google world, if I wanted to explore an interest, it would require finding (and reading) a book/article, and then possibly continuing this search online. This seemed like a lot of work to the sixteen- to seventeen-year-old me (yes, I was a bit lazy), so I put up a wall and I went through the motions in school as so many students do.

But I had a teacher, Mr. Flynn. He was one of my favorite teachers, who just happened to teach one of my least favorite subjects: math. Math had never come easily to me the way many English and social studies classes had, and so I usually retreated from trying and did just enough to get by. By all accounts, Mr. Flynn should never have taken an interest in my learning journey. I spent most of his pre-calculus class passing notes or laughing at others goofing around.

Then one day we came into class, and Mr. Flynn was lying down on the back table. It seemed like a joke, but eventually we found out he had seriously hurt his back. He taught the rest of that class period lying down, pointing to the chalkboard and using a yard stick to make changes.

Everyone thought he would be gone the next day, resting up at home. But sure enough, when we walked into class the following day, Mr. Flynn was again lying on the table and ready to teach. There are certain moments in life where your mindset switches. I still didn't "like" pre-calculus class, but I wasn't going to goof around anymore while this teacher—in obvious pain—was coming in every day to teach instead of staying at home like so many of us would have done.

It was a whole month before Mr. Flynn was back up again, teaching us from a standing position. One day he came over and asked me if I'd like to take computer programming the following year. He had been teaching it for a few years, but enrollment was low, and he wasn't sure the class would run again.

I didn't know what to say. I was shocked that he thought I would like this class, but I told him I'd think about it. A few days later I signed up, thinking I'd at least have a great teacher even if I didn't like the class.

I took Mr. Flynn's computer programming class during my junior year. It was so different. I've never been a math or numbers person, but this gave numbers and formulas power. Instead of getting a "right answer" on a test for getting a formula correct, programming set things in motion.

We learned Pascal and Basic programming languages. It wasn't that hard, but it was challenging enough that I had to focus and pay attention during class and spend some extra time at night or during study hall to get better.

As a semester course, time was limited, so we had to hurry through the beginning curriculum in order to create our own projects. This, in my opinion, is always a plus. It calls for urgency in the learning process, which makes learners and teachers more effective if they are on the same page.

My final project was using the programming language to build a "football" game that looked and functioned similarly to the famous Nintendo Tecmo Bowl.

I spent a lot of time on this (so much that I did not realize how much time I spent). In the end, my football game was not fully functional (there was no end of the game, let alone a halftime or quarter). But it did have many of the same features and abilities as Tecmo Bowl, and my classmates and I were able to play it.

IT WAS AWESOME!

I went through the rest of high school still worrying about the same things, but my outlook on learning was changed forever. When I got to college, I spent more time on "side projects" than ever before. The experience lead me to become the type of learner and teacher I am today.

I tell this story because too often we fail to let students or employees "scratch an itch." I would never have learned the math or formulas needed unless I had to program that game.

It was the interest and final product that had me learning on my own time at a rapid pace. Mr. Flynn never worked to "engage" me during programming class. Instead, he let the creative process fuel my work and empowered me to be a maker instead of only a learner.

IT STARTED WITH STUDENT ENGAGEMENT.

I've always remembered how Mr. Flynn's actions of going above and beyond engaged me as a student in his math class. It built our teacher-student relationship in ways a conversation never could. I had the ultimate respect for him and what he brought to class every day.

In my first year of teaching at Wissahickon Middle School, I had the opportunity to work with an amazing veteran teacher, Jen Smith, who took me under her wing. One of the best things about working with Jen was her consistent goal of making the learning engaging in our classrooms.

We both taught English Language Arts on the same eighth grade team. When we would meet to plan, Jen would often say, "So this is how we did it last year, but I want to make it better. Is there any way we can use technology or some other idea to make it more engaging?"

Jen would ask for us to Look, Listen, and Learn (Phase 1 of the LAUNCH Cycle) before we started to Ask Questions (Phase 2). In one particular situation, we were struggling with literary devices.

We began to empathize with our students, which led us to ask questions like the following:

Why would our students care about literary devices?

What would be the best way to learn the devices?

What would be the best way to assess their learning without regurgitation?

How can we engage the students in understanding their purpose and use in the real world?

As we answered these questions and looked at the work from previous years, we began to Understand the Problem (Phase 3).

Literary devices had always been seen as boring. They were never presented as something exciting, but just something to check off the list of having learned in eighth grade (and needed on the state standardized tests).

We started to brainstorm and Navigate Ideas (Phase 4) on how we could teach the devices in engaging ways. One of our co-teachers offered a piece of advice. She noticed that popular songs always had literary devices in their lyrics.

With that, we started to Create (Phase 5) our very own rap song called, "Welcome to Your Lit Device Education." We had so much fun. As a team of teachers (most well into their careers), we created "Rapper names" and wrote a song script with lit devices, and I added a few beats from Garage Band. Then we worked for hours Highlighting what worked and what didn't and fixing the lyrics and song (Phase 6). We recorded it and then put it online. Finally, we shared it with our students (Phase 7: the LAUNCH) and watched as they not only laughed hysterically at us, but also began to put the song on their iPods and listen to it at home. Here's the song: bit.ly/2qiezVy. Even though I'm really embarrassed, it's fun to look back on this experience of solving a problem by collaborating and creating with colleagues.

DESIGN THINKING WAS A GREAT START, BUT IT WASN'T ENOUGH.

We love design thinking. We wrote a book on it. We talk about it **ALL THE TIME**. We geek out on it. We use it in our teaching, leading, and creative work. But it's only a framework, and the framework alone is not enough.

EMPOWERING MAKERS IN MY CLASSROOM

Our students were engaged, and they were focused on literary devices, but Jen wouldn't let us stop there. Our students now wanted to use programs like Garage Band, YouTube, Audacity, and others to make their own podcasts, songs, and videos.

THIS IS THE JUMP.

For a while, my only focus was on engaging students. We did this as teachers by making the learning meaningful, relevant, social, and human. We made connections with our students and challenged them at the right levels to see high attention and high commitment.

But when we allowed our students to make their own podcasts and songs, made time for them to create and fail along the way, supported their work as guides, and then praised the effort and process—it empowered them as makers.

When our students went through the LAUNCH Cycle themselves and used the design-thinking process as a framework for creative work, they were not only engaged in what they were learning but enthusiastic about what they were making for a real audience.

CREATIVITY ALONE ISN'T ENOUGH IF YOU WANT TRANSFORMATION, YOU NEED TO HAVE STUDENT OWNERSHIP.

TRANSFORMATION

DESIGN THINKING

STUDENT OWNERSHIP

ARE YOU WILLING TO MAKE THE JUMP?

Mr. Flynn had already won me over as a student when he taught on the table with a bad back—for a month. But it was the lessons and activities and projects we did in computer programming class that really made me appreciate him as a teacher and guide.

Similarly, our students thought we were hilarious and appreciated the time and effort we put into making that song about literary devices.

But when we empowered them to make, create, and build their own podcasts and songs, their learning was transformed.

My hope is that all of us can, like Mr. Flynn, empower our students on top of engaging them, and ultimately that we can impact our students' lives the way he impacted mine. I never told Mr. Flynn how much his teaching—while lying on a table—and inviting me to a computer programming class meant to me. Like Mr. Flynn, we can be a part of changing students' lives, often without even knowing it happened.

Visit EmpowerBook.co to get practical resources for empowering our learners. Join the discussion online using the hashtag #empowerbook.

CHAPTER 4

STUDENT CHOICE IS THE HEARTBEAT OF OWNERSHIP AND EMPOWERMENT.

IT'S A SHIFT FROM "REQUIRE" TO "DESIRE."

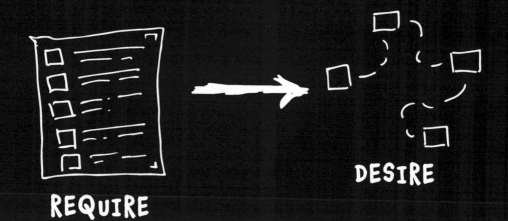

REQUIRE

DESIRE

Students continue to fall into the same trap year after year with traditional schooling. They rarely have a chance to choose their learning path in school and routinely treat school like a "job" instead of the most valuable learning experience they will ever have.

By the time students get to high school, over 83 percent are stressed out, 67 percent say they are bored half the time[9], and many learn to "play the game of school" while worrying about what will happen to them if they do not get a particular grade and get into a specific college.

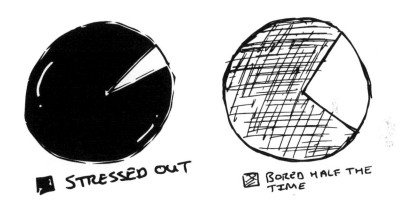

STRESSED OUT

BORED HALF THE TIME

Note that if you fold the page in half and flip it back and forth, you get a stop-animation version of Pac-Man. How cool is that?

We end up with students who are never given a chance to find and develop their passions in school, who end up confused about what they want to do with their lives because they continue to march down a path that has been chosen for them for twelve years. Many of these students end up getting jobs in fields they think are "safe" or "practical" but don't have a personal connection or interest to the work they are doing.

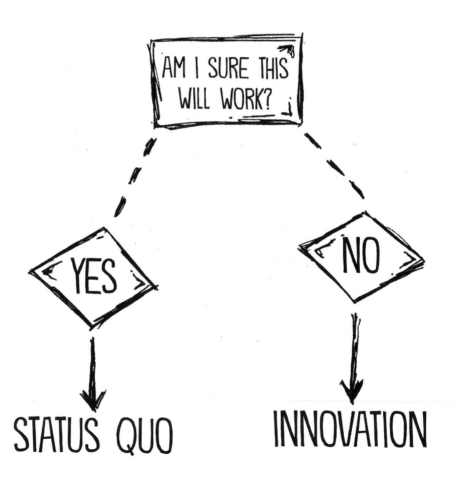

Have you ever met an adult who doesn't like their job? I've met many. And it's not necessarily their fault, our system produces many adults who never had a chance to find their passion through schooling and instead found that the best way to get by was to keep getting by.

But this can change almost immediately if we add one key ingredient to school: choice.

WHY CHOICE MATTERS IN SCHOOL

Choice in what content our students consume, what activities they take on in and out of school, what assessments they take, and choice in their purpose for learning.

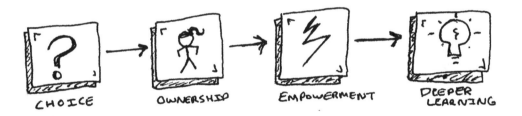

CHOICE → OWNERSHIP → EMPOWERMENT → DEEPER LEARNING

Choice drives student ownership of their learning. This kicks empowerment into high gear, and ultimately leads to learning that is intrinsic, powerful, and deep.

I (A.J.) have seen this change firsthand. A few years ago, I gave my students choice in the form of a 20% Time project. Just as Google gave their engineers 20 percent of their time to work on whatever they were passionate about, I gave my students 20 percent of our class time to learn, research, make, and create something about which they were passionate.

Many of my students were blinded by the choice at first. It was difficult for them to find their way without a rubric, a project handout, or guidelines to move them forward. But eventually, they began to learn about things in which they were interested, and the products they created gave each a purpose for deep learning.

But choice does not have to be given every time with the pure freedom of a 20% Time or Genius Hour Project.

Limitations often inspire more creativity. They become the creative constraint that leads to innovative breakthroughs.

Studying photosynthesis in class? Give students a variety of content choices to learn the basics, then ask them to demonstrate their knowledge through making a video, giving an oral presentation, conducting a podcast interview, or creating an infographic (using paper or computer).

Choice dictates a sense of ownership and autonomy, even when presented with limitations.

CHANGING THE GAME
OF SCHOOL MEANS
ACTUALLY ALLOWING
STUDENTS TO CREATE
THEIR OWN GAME.

THIS IS EMPOWERMENT.

MORE THAN "TRYING NEW THINGS" IN SCHOOL

Sir Ken Robinson, author of *The Element*, has famously said, "Whether or not you discover your talents and passions is partly a matter of opportunity. If you've never been sailing, or picked up an instrument, or tried to teach or to write fiction, how would you know if you had a talent for these things?"

And I would take this thought a step further. Schools pride themselves on giving students all types of opportunities.

Many educators (myself included) believe that education is the bridge that allows someone to do what they love for a living and love what they do for a living.

Yet the problem is that we often fail to **encourage** students to try new things and instead **demand** that they try new things. It may sound like a small difference, but let me tell you, it has huge ramifications. Encouraging expands options and affirms student agency. Demanding limits options and pushes compliance.

Dale Carnegie[10] points out the following:

"PERSONALLY I AM VERY FOND OF STRAWBERRIES AND CREAM, BUT I HAVE FOUND THAT FOR SOME STRANGE REASON, FISH PREFER WORMS."

We can't predict what will catch our students' attention. We can't choose what will engage them. And we can't force them to have high attention and commitment in their learning if there is no chance for ownership.

Choice gives students the opportunity to cast their own line and choose what bait they want to put on the hook. Learning follows, not because it is forced upon them, but because it is naturally connected to curiosity and inquiry.

To reinvent school, we don't need to scrap the entire system. We don't need to start from scratch. We don't need to throw away what has worked. Instead, we need to change our focus from rigor to vigor.

Choice, whether completely free or with limitations, is what will drive our students to dive deeper into learning. And it may bring us back to why we loved learning in the first place: It allows us to do the things we can only dream of doing.

Remember, the shift is simple: Our job as teachers is not to prepare students for "something;" our job is to help students to prepare themselves for anything. Let them choose, and watch what they can do.

Visit EmpowerBook.co to get practical resources for empowering our learners. Join the discussion online using the hashtag #empowerbook.

CHAPTER 5

IT'S NOT ABOUT GIVING THEM A
ROADMAP FOR LEARNING. IT'S
ABOUT HELPING THEM CREATE
THEIR OWN MAPS.

WE NEED TO SHIFT FROM PROVIDING CHOICES TO INSPIRING POSSIBILITIES

It was my (John) first year of teaching, and this was supposed to be my greatest lesson of the school year. I had planned it for hours, revising every element until it looked flawless.

On paper.

But suddenly, in third period, the reality sank in. My lesson sucked. Students weren't engaged. They didn't want to create Civil War newspapers.

A few students looked engaged on the surface. They were listening, answering discussion questions, and participating. A few of them even got excited about drawing Civil War political cartoons. Still, I knew something was missing.

MY STUDENTS DIDN'T OWN THE LEARNING.

At the time, I viewed teaching as a content delivery system. I worked tirelessly to create content that would be meaningful, fun, and challenging. When students seemed disinterested, I would try and dress it up with more humor or a pop culture twist.

But it was always **my content**, and I was always the person delivering it.

CONTENT DELIVERY MODEL:

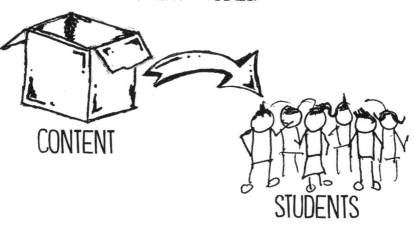

CONTENT

STUDENTS

Don't get me wrong. Students completed projects. But these were culminating projects at the end of a unit. To be honest, they weren't really projects. They were more like crafts.

Our classroom projects looked nothing like the kinds of projects people do outside of school. I had strict rules on everything from formatting to strategies to pace to style. I handed students project papers that were essentially paint-by-number instructions. It never occurred to me that students could paint their own pictures.

I had the best of intentions. I wanted students to know what they were supposed to do. So I provided clear instructions telling them what to do. But I left out a critical ingredient: choice.

Looking back at it, I realize that these projects had always been about me.

Here's what I mean:

I CHOSE THE RESOURCES.
I CHOSE THE CONTENT.
I ASKED THE QUESTIONS.
I WROTE THE INSTRUCTIONS.
I MANAGED THE PROJECT PROGRESS.
I CHOSE THE TASKS.
I WROTE THE OBJECTIVES.
I PICKED THE STANDARDS.
I DECIDED ON THE FORMAT.
I DETERMINED WHETHER OR NOT THE WORK WAS ANY GOOD.

In other words, I chose everything ahead of time.

I WAS AFRAID.

Even though I (John) wanted my students to have creative control, I was terrified. I knew I believed in student choice, but there were too many doubts floating around in my head.

MY PRINCIPAL MIGHT
JUDGE ME FOR THIS

THEY MIGHT FAIL THE TEST

I COULDN'T PREDICT WHERE
WE WERE GOING

IT MIGHT NOT
FIT THE STANDARDS

IT MIGHT GET TOO LOUD

THESE WERE
MY FEARS

KIDS MIGHT TALK
THE WHOLE TIME

THINGS MIGHT GET
CHAOTIC

IT MIGHT TAKE UP
TOO MUCH TIME

KIDS MIGHT BE OFF-TASK

STUDENTS MIGHT
STOP WORKING

I WOULDN'T BE ABLE TO
TRACK HOW MY STUDENTS WERE DOING

IT FELT LIKE A GAMBLE

THE TOURIST TRAP

Looking back on it, I see I was acting like a tour guide, leading my students through the content. Each lesson was a carefully packaged presentation where I would entertain my students and point out areas of interest. A few students might ask questions and, on a good day, we would have a discussion.

But we never left the tour bus. We stuck tightly to the route spelled out by the curriculum map, stopping every few days to take on a new standard and tackle a new objective.

I WAS A TOURIST TEACHER

AN ACCURATE DEPICTION OF MY RECEDING HAIRLINE

SMILE: I WAS THE ONLY ONE EXCITED

ITINERARY: I DECIDED THE PACE AND PROCESS

CAMERA: I WAS THE ONLY ONE DOCUMENTING THE LEARNING

FANNY PACK: I HANDLED THE RESOURCES

MAP: I CHOSE WHERE WE WENT

HIGH SOCKS: I TRIED TO BE RELEVANT BUT I WAS LIKE THE DUDE WEARING HIGH SOCKS AND SANDALS

When students were bored, I doubled down on the entertainment factor. When they were confused, I simplified my explanations. But we were all going in the same direction at the same pace in the same way.

And I was the one driving the instruction bus.

THEN EVERYTHING CHANGED.

It was a "lame duck" week during state testing. I had one social studies class for three hours each day, and we didn't have a curriculum map.

So I asked my students a simple question: "What do you want to make?"

After a short class discussion, we landed on a documentary project about immigration. Students formed small groups and began researching the topic. What happened next was a mess. I gave mini-lessons on how to conduct interviews, how to shoot video, and how to tell a non-fiction story. I met with students one-on-one to go over how to find more credible sources. We shared scripts back and forth on a shared document.

But things didn't go smoothly. A few students didn't finish their parts. We never launched it to a real audience. Some of my highest performing students were more frustrated and more afraid than ever before. They had never failed like this. A few kids were in tears when they couldn't get something to work.

Still, something emerged from the mess.

My students were different.

Students who had never turned in homework before began voluntarily shooting videos of immigrants in their neighborhoods. Students who had never asked questions in class were asking hard-hitting interview questions. Students who had once told me, "I'm not very creative" were setting up storyboards and editing videos.

They were literally making history by recording interviews, adding their own scripts, finding visuals, and then working collaboratively with other teams to create one larger documentary.

They were also empowered. They were excited. They were passionate. They were makers.

Everything changed!

The secret ingredient wasn't a new maker space or a fancy studio. (My students shot the videos on their cell phones.) It wasn't a new program or a district initiative. No, the secret ingredient was *freedom*. Without the curriculum map, we were forced to go off road. And although the road was rocky (*hmm … rocky road*) it was also an epic adventure.

I spent the next summer analyzing every part of my classroom with a single driving question:

WHAT DECISIONS AM I MAKING FOR STUDENTS THAT THEY COULD MAKE FOR THEMSELVES?

It was humbling. I realized that I was working like crazy while my students were bored—or, at best, entertained. That's when I revamped everything—my class rules, procedures, instructional strategies, lesson plans, projects, and assessments.

Everything.

I decided we would go off road. I made a list of every possible way for students to own the process. Here are key areas I came up with.

#1: STUDENTS WOULD DECIDE ON THE DESTINATION

Instead of sticking to the same rigid routes, I would let students explore the content. They would decide on the topics and the sub-topics based upon their own geeky (or non-geeky) interests.

I knew that I still had to teach specific content. We had standards and curriculum maps. But I quickly realized that a curriculum map is just that—a map. And maps should inspire possibilities rather than limit options. We'll be exploring this idea later in the chapter.

#2: STUDENTS WOULD ASK THE QUESTIONS

Instead of answering a set of predetermined questions, students would ask their own questions based upon their own curiosity. Sometimes they would go out on their own and chase a question. Other times, they would ask questions of one another and explore ideas as a group. But they would own the inquiry process.

#3: STUDENTS WOULD SET THE PACE

The tourist approach requires everyone to stay together in a group. But off road, students can work at their own pace. Some blaze a trail quickly. Others take their time as they learn the new terrain. But nobody has to be "left behind." It's not a race or a contest. It's an epic adventure.

#4: STUDENTS WOULD SELECT THE TOOLS

Instead of requiring students to finish specific activities, they have the option of using whatever tools they find helpful. So maybe one student needs notecards. Another prefers a spreadsheet. They would own the tools and decide on the strategies as they engage in the projects.

#5: STUDENTS WOULD SELECT THE LEARNING TARGETS

Although we often had a shared-classroom learning target for the day, students could self-select additional learning targets depending upon their own need for intervention or enrichment. All scaffolding would be optional and students would self-select it.

WHO DRIVES
THE LEARNING
IN YOUR
CLASSROOM?

I was terrified.

I was afraid that students would be lazy. Instead, they worked harder because they cared about their work. I was afraid they would get confused and give up. Instead, they took more creative risks. I was worried we wouldn't get to all the standards. Instead, students spent more time on the skills they needed to hone and less on the ones they needed to master. I was terrified of the test, but we always remained in the top half of the test scores.

It didn't always work perfectly. I had projects that tanked. I had moments when I over-edited and acted like one of those parents who gives too much help in a project. We had moments when students were rushed and didn't finish at all. We had too much structure and then not enough structure. And even on the best days, there were some students who were feeling unmotivated.

Even now, I'm still on this journey of student choice. I still talk too much in class. I still make too many decisions. I still have a hard time letting students self-manage. But I'm convinced that the answer is to empower students by giving them more voice and choice in what they're learning.

WHAT ABOUT THE CURRICULUM MAP?

Going off road is great, but here's the reality: We all have standards and curriculum maps and rules about what we have to cover on specific days. Most of us work in factory-styled, standardized systems where students are supposed to do the same thing at the same time in the same way at the same pace.

In other words, the system isn't designed for epic adventures. This is where you get to be creative. A curriculum map is exactly that—a map. And maps should inspire possibilities rather than limit options.

Chances are that your curriculum map will tell you that you need to hit specific standards on specific days. But that's just the starting point. Sometimes you have to find the hidden opportunities.

Here's what we mean:

1. Take note of content-neutral standards that allow students to choose the topic.

2. Show that student inquiry and research are actually a chance to dive deeper into the content area while also practicing the skill-based standards in language arts and problem solving in math.

3. While the curriculum map sets the pace for specific standards, it doesn't mean students can't practice certain standards in order to reach mastery. This is simply embedded intervention.

4. Remember that the curriculum map tells you what you have to teach. **But it doesn't tell you what you can't teach.** If students are self-selecting standards and practicing skills they desperately need, you can point to this as embedded intervention. You can point out that this is hitting both the Spiral Learning Model and the Mastery Model at the same time.

WHEN STUDENTS CHOOSE THE ROUTE, THEY LEARN HOW TO NAVIGATE THEIR OWN LEARNING.

IMAGINE YOU'RE A STUDENT ...

Picture yourself as an eighth-grade science student. The current unit is about the scientific method as well as forces and motion. In other classes, the teacher gives a PowerPoint presentation while students take notes. Eventually, the teacher gives a demonstration. Then, finally, every student follows a recipe-style lab and writes the same kind of write-up.

But your class is different. It starts out with questions. You play around with objects and ask questions about things like rate and movement and gravity. You work with a group of four students doing research. Here you get to read at your own pace and at your own level. Even though you struggle with informational reading, you are able to find help through a series of videos that explain the scientific concepts. At one point, your teacher sits down with you to help you identify important facts from the text.

During this process, your small group creates a short video answering one of your inquiry questions. After a period of playing around and researching, the teacher gives you a scenario.

You will be designing model roller coasters. Suddenly, you're applying the ideas you learned in your research and then testing things out, reading more informational text, and eventually applying those ideas to new prototypes. Finally, your class has a competition to see which roller coaster would work best in a new amusement park.

Visit EmpowerBook.co to get practical resources for empowering our learners. Join the discussion online using the hashtag #empowerbook.

CHAPTER 6

STUDENT OWNERSHIP
IS A MINDSET.

IT'S A SHIFT FROM A COMPLIANT MINDSET TO A SELF-DIRECTED MINDSET.

COMPLIANT

SELF-DIRECTED

Not long ago, you could follow a formula. Work hard, study hard, go to college, and climb the corporate ladder.

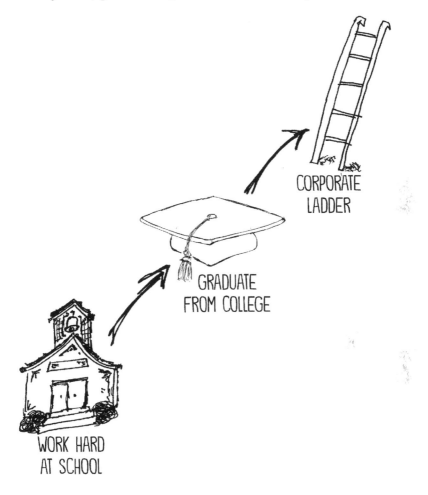

CORPORATE
LADDER

GRADUATE
FROM COLLEGE

WORK HARD
AT SCHOOL

It wasn't about choice or passion or interests. It was about compliance. It was about putting in your time so that you could make it in the world. And it worked—not for everybody and not all the time—for enough people that society embraced it.

BUT THINGS ARE CHANGING.

We live in an era where robotics and artificial intelligence will replace many of our current jobs. Global connectivity will continue to allow companies to outsource labor to other countries. The corporate ladder is gone and in its place is a complex maze.

Our current students will enter a workforce where instability is the new normal and where they will have to be self-directed, original, and creative in order to navigate this maze.

This is a terrifying reality.

And yet . . .

THERE IS A HIDDEN OPPORTUNITY IN ALL OF IT. TRUE, THE RULES HAVE CHANGED. BUT THAT ALSO MEANS STUDENTS CAN REWRITE THE RULES.

We often hear that our current students will work in jobs that don't exist right now. But here's another reality: Our current students will be the ones who create those jobs.

Not every student will create the next Google or Pixar or Lyft. Some students will be engineers or artists or accountants. Some will work in technology, others in traditional corporate spaces and still others in social or civic spaces. But no matter how diverse their industries will be, our students will all someday face a common reality: **Every single one of them will need to think like an entrepreneur in order to thrive in a changing world.** They may not invent a company, but they will have to invent and reinvent their jobs in order to stay relevant. In other words, they'll need to be nimble.

For this reason, we've spent the last few years interviewing entrepreneurs in a wide range of industries. The two questions I've asked each time have been, "What do you wish you had learned in school?" and, "What are the required skills to thrive as an entrepreneur?" Over time, we've come to believe that it's less about a set of transferable skills and more about a mindset. This is why I've started asking, "What does it mean to think like an entrepreneur?"

THE MOST COMMON ANSWER IS, "YOU HAVE TO BE A SELF-STARTER."

NOT EVERY STUDENT WILL BECOME AN ENTREPRENEUR, BUT THEY WILL ALL SOMEDAY NEED TO THINK LIKE ONE.

In other words, entrepreneurs stand out because they don't wait their turn. They don't wait for an opportunity. They don't hope to be called on. They don't expect an instruction manual. They are self-starters who turn an idea into a reality, then into a business. They write their own rules.

But they aren't a special breed of people. In fact, as Adam Grant points out, they are just as scared as you and I. But (and this is key) they are more scared of what will happen if they don't pursue an idea than if they fail.

Students need to be self-starters.

It doesn't end there. Starting something is one thing. Many great ideas fizzle out within a few months when people lose interest.

There's an often overlooked gritty and difficult side to entrepreneurship that shows up every time you hear people use the phrase "It's a grind." They are usually referring to the hard work of being a self-manager. If being a self-starter is all about sparking innovation in the midst of chaos, self-management is all about knowing how to stick to deadlines and routines.

Students need to be self-managers.

SELF-STARTING WITHOUT SELF-MANAGING EQUALS UNFINISHED WORK

THAT LACKS FOLLOW-THROUGH.

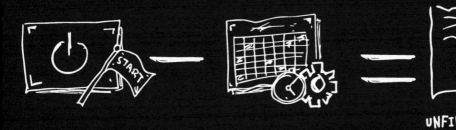

SELF-MANAGING WITHOUT SELF-STARTING EQUALS UNINSPIRED WORK
THAT LACKS INNOVATION.

We often use the expression "self-directed learners" to describe a similar mindset. That phrase encompasses being both a self-starter and a self-manager.

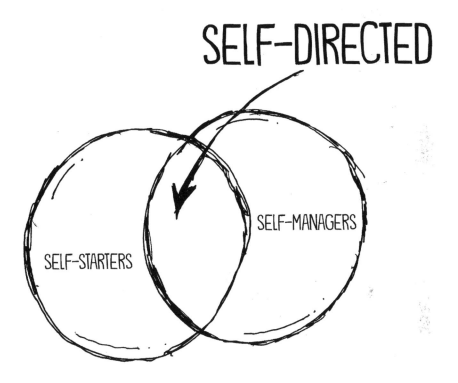

So let's explore these two key components of a self-directed mindset.

PART ONE:

STUDENTS AS
SELF-STARTERS

I (John) once taught an eighth-grade student who had written four novels online, despite the fact that she had only been learning English for three years. She spent her free time in class looking up how to set up lead magnets for an email list. She read blog posts about how to create more suspense in a plot and how to use actions rather than descriptions to develop characters.

She was a self-starter.

I once had a student who taught himself how to code by playing around with Scratch when he was in the sixth grade. With the help of a teacher who mentored him along the way, he became the first child in his family to graduate high school. And now he's working on a master's degree in engineering.

He was a self-starter.

But I also taught students with immense talent who never pursued their dreams because they were waiting for an invitation that never came. They were compliant and well behaved, but they weren't self-starters. So they continued for years, waiting for an offer that never materialized.

SO HOW DO WE ENCOURAGE STUDENTS TO BECOME SELF-STARTERS?

#1: INSPIRE THEM.

Students will take initiative when something matters to them. This sounds simple, but it's actually a challenge. It requires teachers to tap into students' interests and passions. It involves making the subject accessible enough that students feel that they can take charge.

It's that magical thing that happens when students get so excited about an idea they learn in your class that they pursue it on their own at home.

#2: CREATE OPPORTUNITIES FOR SELF-STARTING.

Carve out time in your schedule where students can self-start on their own learning. It might be an inquiry driven Wonder Day or it might be a longer Genius Hour / 20 % Time project. It might involve students blogging, where they choose the genre, the topic, and the format.

#3: PROVIDE THE TOOLS.

Sometimes students have an idea of something they want to learn, but they lack the tools, resources, or materials to make it happen. But when teachers provide the tools, students are able to take the initiative and build something, learn something, or pursue something that had previously been unimaginable.

#4: ENCOURAGE CREATIVE RISK-TAKING.

Fear is the biggest barrier to self-starting. It might be the fear of failure, the fear of not doing it the right way, or the fear that others might not like your work. So students end up having an idea of something they want to learn, but they never pursue it. As a teacher, you can battle this by encouraging creative risk-taking.

#5: MODEL THE THINKING PROCESS.

Show your students how you are self-starting in your own life. If you're writing a novel, tell your students about it and share your fears and struggles as well. Allow them to see that self-starters aren't people with an immense ego or unwavering self-confidence. Let them inside of your head to see how self-starters not only look for opportunities but also create them.

#6: AFFIRM IT.

Point out when you see students taking charge and self-starting their own learning. It might be something as small as choosing their own enrichment activity when they finish early or finding some geeky interest and running with it. But when you see those moments of self-direction, celebrate it! Those little habits lead to that self-starting mindset.

#7: HELP THEM FIND A COMMUNITY.

Self-starters aren't lone rangers. They are often connected to peers and mentors who help them navigate the process. The same is true of students. At an older age, this might mean a shadowing opportunity or the introduction of a guest speaker. At a younger age, it might mean helping parents or guardians find venues where students can pursue these interests on their own.

PART TWO:
STUDENTS AS
SELF-MANAGERS

The second half of this mindset is self-managing. It's the idea of following through on your plans and continuing with tasks even when nobody is looking over your shoulder.

This is the part that's often described as a "grind" by entrepreneurs; however, it's also where we get the chance to see our results and meet our goals. It's where the real work is found. The following are some of the key components.

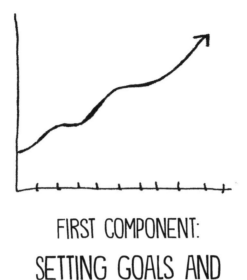

FIRST COMPONENT:
SETTING GOALS AND
CHARTING PROGRESS

Self-management begins with a sense of awareness regarding what you are doing, where you are going, and what you plan to do next. Students with this sense of awareness understand not only what they are doing but why they are doing it.

With a strong sense of what they are doing and where they are going, students begin to set goals. These might be learning goals or project goals. They then monitor their progress and reflect often on how they are doing and what they need to do next in order to improve.

SECOND COMPONENT:
BREAKING DOWN TASKS AND SETTING DEADLINES

Self-managers are able to take a larger task and break it down into sub-tasks and eventually deadlines. They can think realistically about what is needed in terms of time, resources, and concrete actions. This is a critical piece of project management. It requires students to see the big picture, the details, and the complex relationship between the two.

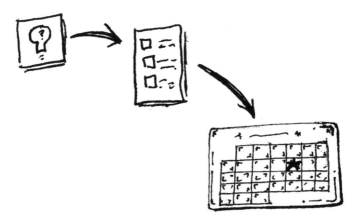

Often teachers will set up external deadlines for various phases in a project. But this can actually shortcut the vital skill of project management. When students are able to break tasks down and set realistic deadlines, they are able to turn a project from an idea into a reality.

THIRD COMPONENT:
PROBLEM SOLVING AND FLEXIBLE THINKING

While tasks and deadlines are vital to self-management, things will not always work according to plan. Students can have the best-developed plans in the world, but ultimately life will happen. But then the internet goes down for a day. A group member gets sick for two days. You have a fire drill and then an unplanned assembly. A few students hit a creative block and suddenly feel stuck. In these moments, students will need to solve problems and deal with issues as they arise. Things will break. Plans will change. This is the frustrating side of student-centered learning. It's messier than a tidy worksheet. And yet, when students are able to tackle these challenges, they grow into problem solvers and critical thinkers.

FOURTH COMPONENT:

CHOOSING STRATEGIES

Self-managers are able to determine what strategies they will use in order to complete their tasks. They can select the resources and materials while also deciding on the processing that will work best for them. So when doing research, they might use notecards or a spreadsheet.

When managing their project, they might keep their tasks on a shared document or on a shared calendar. But in these moments, they move from using strategies—because the teacher told them to do it—and toward choosing strategies because it helps them accomplish their goals.

THIS REQUIRES REAL PROJECTS.

It's not surprising that this type of self-management is so similar to project management (which is a job that will always be needed in a complex economy). You can't learn this type of self-management with packets of worksheets. If we want students to develop this mindset, they need to work on projects.

Real projects.

The kinds of projects that matter to them. The kind where they are in the driver's seat. And that's why students need to own the creative process.

Visit EmpowerBook.co to get practical resources for empowering our learners. Join the discussion online using the hashtag #empowerbook.

CHAPTER 7

EVERY STUDENT IS A MAKER.

THE SHIFT
FROM CONSUMING
TO CREATING

Actually, consuming isn't all bad.
We'll get into that in a little bit.

A few years back, I (John) surveyed my students to see how they used their devices (tablets, laptops, and smartphones). Were they consuming or creating? Here were the results:

CONSUME | CREATE

WATCH A VIDEO

158 OF 160

CREATE AND EDIT A VIDEO

4 OF 160

LISTEN TO AUDIO

160 OF 160

CREATE AND EDIT AUDIO

3 OF 160

PLAYED A VIDEO GAME

153 OF 160

CREATE A VIDEO GAME

0 OF 160

I had a group of three or four students who were outliers. They were the ones I mentioned in the last chapter. One student wrote novels. Another had a thriving YouTube channel. One kid had a podcast. I realized that the real divide wasn't a digital divide.

It was a creative chasm—a break between the consumers and creators, the makers and the takers. And although "taker" might sound a bit extreme, I couldn't help but remember the words of my former teacher, Mrs. Smoot:

"WE ROB THE WORLD OF OUR CREATIVITY WHEN WE NEVER MAKE ANYTHING."

As my former students move into college and step into careers, I notice that the makers are better equipped for life. They are taking ownership of their careers and forging a way into whatever vocation they have chosen. But this goes beyond economics. The makers have better endurance and deeper thinking. They know how to handle frustration.

THEY WERE THE
MAKERS
BUILDING A
BETTER FUTURE AND
CHANGING
THE WORLD.

WE WANT STUDENTS TO BE INNOVATORS.

In the previous chapter, we mentioned the uncertain world our students will inhabit. But the makers are the ones who are thriving. They're the ones who are experimenting and taking creative risks. They're thinking divergently.

In other words, they're innovators.

Here's a quick confession: I (John) used to hate the word "innovative." See those quotation marks right there around the word? Those are actually air quotes that I would use whenever I used the term.

"It's a buzzword," I would say.

"It's overused," I would point out.

But the truth is, sometimes a word becomes trendy because it's tapping into something we all agree is important. Is it misused? Sometimes. Is it overused? Often. But so are the words "love" and "awesome" and "friend," but I have no intention of ditching any of those words.

I think I reacted poorly to the word "innovation" because it had a certain overly glossy, high-tech connotation to it. It made me think of the EPCOT Center and of the Astrodome and of the Flowbee (a true innovation in haircutting that combined a hair trimmer and a vacuum).

94

But that's not innovation. That's novelty. That's disruption.

That's change for the sake of change.

Innovation is different.

Innovation is what Lin Manuel Miranda did with *Hamilton* and what Gabriel Garcia Marquez accomplished decades ago with magical realism. Innovation is Camden Yards and AT&T Ballpark, boldly changing ballparks by incorporating the vintage rather than trying to build a new Astrodome. Innovation is that cancer treatment that didn't exist five years ago but now has the chance to save the life of a friend you love.

Innovation isn't change for the sake of change. It's driven by a sense of purpose and meaning. It's what happens when you say, "There's got to be a better way," and then you experiment and take creative risks to see what happens. It's what happens when you ask, "Why not?" and challenge the status quo because there is a problem you care deeply about, and you're determined to solve it.

I know the term might be trendy and maybe even overused, but I want to see innovation in our schools. I want to see our students grow into innovators. I want to see them engage in divergent thinking as they find new routes to solve complex problems. I want to see them take creative risks and challenge the status quo. I want to see them be boldly and unabashedly different. I want to see them be innovative.

BE WILDLY AND
UNABASHEDLY DIFFERENT.

IF WE WANT STUDENTS TO **INNOVATE** IN THE FUTURE, WE NEED THEM TO OWN THE PROCESS **NOW.**

IT'S ABOUT THE MAKING, NOT THE SPACE.

When I go back to that story from eighth grade, I am reminded that it's not about the latest gadgets. After all, I was cutting audio tape with a razor. I was making long-distance phone calls. The technology changed, but the maker mindset lasted forever.

It's easy to fixate on maker spaces and the perfect creative environment. And yet, it's not about the physical space. After all, we want students to be creative anywhere at any time.

It's about the teachers, the relationships, and the power of equipping students to become creative thinkers. But this requires students to own the creative process.

OWNING THE CREATIVE PROCESS

There's a time and a place to tell students to "go make something." We've found success with rapid prototyping, divergent-thinking exercises, and quick-thinking, creative problem solving.

But we also know that sometimes creative work is slower. It takes time to plan things out and develop solutions. You need a certain level of mental slack to wander through ideas and experiment with options and ultimately design a solution.

Moreover, sometimes creative work requires structure. Students often struggle with a completely open process. They rush into creating something new without thinking about planning or purpose, and then they're disappointed with the results. They have a tough time getting started.

Structure isn't a bad thing if it promotes student choice. Sometimes you need a framework for your creative work or a road map to help you along the way. You still get to make the decisions, but the structure actually amplifies the creative work.

This is why we're passionate about design thinking. It's a structure that empowers, rather than limits, student ownership.

Design thinking is a flexible framework designed to get the most out of the creative process. It's used in a diverse range of industries: the corporate world, social and civic spaces, and higher education.

The structure enhances rather than inhibits student voice and choice. When students engage in design thinking, they own the entire creative process.

Design thinking works within the standards in every subject. It's a flexible approach that you can use with limited resources. It isn't something new that you add to your crowded schedule. Instead, it's an innovative approach to the work you are already doing—a process designed specifically to boost creativity and bring out the maker in every student.

This is why we developed the student-friendly LAUNCH Cycle. It's a design thinking framework specifically tailored to K–12 classrooms that you can use at any grade level. Think of it this way. Making is the mindset. Design thinking is the process. The LAUNCH Cycle is the framework.

MAKING IS THE MINDSET   DESIGN THINKING IS THE PROCESS   LAUNCH IS THE FRAMEWORK

Let's explore how LAUNCH empowers students at every stage of the process.

PHASE ONE
L: LOOK, LISTEN, AND LEARN.

In the first phase, students look, listen, and learn. The goal here is awareness. It might be a sense of wonder at a process or an awareness of a problem or a sense of empathy toward an audience. Regardless of where they start, students begin with their own awareness.

From the very first phase, the creative process is student driven by tapping into their questions, their own sense of wonder, or their empathy toward an audience. So while the teacher might provide an initial prompt or experience, the goal is to tap into each student's own sense of curiosity.

PHASE TWO
A: ASK TONS OF QUESTIONS.

Sparked by curiosity, students move to the second phase where they ask tons of questions. These might be questions about a process, a system, or a physical phenomenon. They might be questions that students ask as a needs assessment to grow in empathy toward an audience, or they might be research questions.

But the key thing is that students are asking the questions.

Notice that they are not answering a set of teacher questions or linking back to essential questions developed during unit planning. Instead, they are engaged in their own inquiry process.

PHASE THREE
U: UNDERSTAND THE PROCESS OR PROBLEM.

This leads to understanding the process or problem through an authentic research experience. They might conduct interviews or needs assessments, research articles, watch videos, or analyze data. This is a choice-driven research process, where students are selecting the resources, finding the information, and using the strategies they find useful.

In this phase, students own the research process. They are answering the questions they generated in the previous phase. They choose the sources and the format for their research and ultimately that leads to a greater sense of background knowledge which helps them in the next phase.

PHASE FOUR
N: NAVIGATE IDEAS.

Students apply that newly acquired knowledge to potential solutions. In this phase, they navigate ideas. Here they brainstorm, analyze, and combine ideas and generate a concept for what they will create. They can work individually or collaboratively as they move through this ideation process.

Instead of following a project sheet with a recipe-style list of steps, students create their own solution and then develop a plan of action. They own the ideas and the process.

Students get a chance to own the project management from generating the ideas through developing a plan and then ultimately through creating their prototype.

PHASE FIVE
C: CREATE A PROTOTYPE.

In this next phase, students create a prototype. It might be a digital work or a tangible product, a work of art or something they engineer. It might even be an action or an event or a system.

But they are driving the process, including what they will make and how they will make it. This part is sometimes messy, slow, and confusing; however, it's also powerful as you watch your students' eyes light up in that moment when something works for the first time.

This is when they see their idea become a reality and where they ultimately define themselves as builders, makers, tinkerers, and designers.

PHASE SIX
H: HIGHLIGHT WHAT WORKS, AND FIX WHAT'S FAILING.

Next they begin to highlight what's working and fix what's failing. The goal here is to view this revision process as an experiment full of iterations, where every mistake takes them closer to success.

They engage in self-assessment, peer assessment, and one-on-one conferencing with the teacher as they refine their work (an idea we'll be exploring in an upcoming chapter).

PHASE SEVEN
LAUNCH TO AN AUDIENCE.

When it's done, it's ready to launch. In the launch phase, they send it to an authentic audience. They share their work with an audience that they have chosen. Over time, their creative confidence grows, and they see the power in sharing their work with the world.

HOW DO WE MAKE THIS HAPPEN?

We know that all children are natural makers. But how do we unleash this creativity in a system where you don't have enough technology, and you lack time, and you have a rigid curriculum map tied to a high-stakes test?

TRY IT FOR ONE DAY.

THAT'S RIGHT.

JUST ONE DAY.

CHOOSE A WASTED DAY, LIKE THE DAY OF STATE TESTING OR THE DAY BEFORE A BREAK OR THE DAY WHEN NOBODY EXPECTS MUCH. HERE ARE A FEW IDEAS YOU COULD TRY.

MAKER CHALLENGES

Maker challenges are short-term projects that focus on rapid prototyping. Students work through the LAUNCH cycle quickly and get a chance to make something physical. The focus is often STEM related, though you can easily do a maker project in other subjects.

Maker challenges begin with a specific problem in mind. In fact, I (John) created a series of animated videos with maker challenges. You can find them at videoprompts.com.

Now here's the beauty of it: You don't need to have the latest and greatest technology to pull off a maker challenge. Some of the best challenges start with some duct tape and cardboard.

Maker challenges don't require much extra time. All they require is a little bit of imagination and a willingness to try something new.

GLOBAL DAY OF DESIGN

A few years back, we decided to launch a global collaboration project. Our goal was simple: Try out design thinking for one day. We chose a "throw away" day toward the end of the semester once testing was over, and teachers had the permission to experiment for just one day.

Just one day.

We knew that wasn't enough.

We knew that a single day wasn't enough to transform classrooms into bastions of creativity and wonder.

BUT IT COULD LIGHT A SPARK.

We watched on social media as teachers collaborated and students shared their work with the world. More than 85,000 students participated. They were scattered on six different continents but tied together by one common goal: make something awesome.

Half the classes didn't have fancy technology. Some of the students weren't able to finish their project.

But it didn't matter. Students were empowered. They were asking the questions. They were generating the ideas. They were building the products.

111

They were makers.

Not because of the Global Day of Design. Not because of design thinking. It was because of their teachers who were bold enough to take creative risks and empower their students to own the creative process.

What began as a single day grew into a movement in certain schools. Teachers ran with design thinking and transformed whole grade levels and eventually entire schools.

A LITTLE
NUANCE
HERE ...

WE ACTUALLY
WANT
STUDENTS
TO BE
CONSUMERS.

Consuming is actually necessary for creativity. Often there's a cycle that goes on where you consume things, and then you're inspired to create. After all, most chefs enjoy great food. Most guitarists love listening to music.

There's an ongoing cycle of critical consuming, inspiration, and creative work.

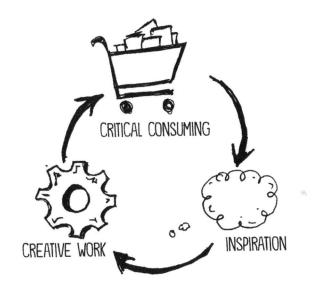

They key thing here is **critical** consuming. And this type of consuming begins with ownership.

See, I (John) used to believe that creativity began in the mind. Ideas popped in and people responded externally by making things. I would get frustrated when students came into class having only used technology to consume rather than create. I would beg them to take risks creatively. Make something different. Be bold. Branch out, even if you screw up.

However, things began to change when I had my own kids. I noticed that from a young age, creativity was inherently social. It often began by seeing, hearing, and experiencing first. Often it included copying something that an adult was doing. As the kids grew older, I noticed a similar pattern. Though they were wildly creative, each one of them went through a process of noticing, exploring, copying, and finally finding their own way.

I have noticed similar trends among students. They often go through a phase of copying and mash-ups that occur before creating something truly original. I see this trend in art class, wood shop, in writer's workshops, and in STEM labs.

So this has me thinking about stages that I notice as students move from consumers to creators.

FIRST STAGE
EXPOSURE (PASSIVE CONSUMING)

Sometimes this is a passive exposure. You hear a style of music being played in the background and it seems unusual. After a few months of it, you find yourself thinking, *I kind of like this.* Next thing you know, you're choosing to listen to indie-fused techno-polka. Or maybe not. Maybe indie-fused techno-polka is a bad idea.

This is a reminder that even in a choice-driven classroom, there is still value in exposing students to new ideas, new content, and new experiences. And sometimes students might not enjoy a particular book or topic or even subject until you've introduced it to them.

Other times, it's more direct. You watch a particular movie, or you see a production, or you read a book, and suddenly you're hooked. That's when you move into the second phase.

SECOND STAGE
ACTIVE CONSUMING

In this phase, you are more likely to seek out the works that you are consuming (whether it is art, music, food, or poetry). You aren't yet a fan, but you start developing a taste for a particular style and you find yourself thinking more deeply about whatever work you are consuming.

Sometimes this phase is more focused on the aesthetics, and sometimes it is more focused on practical utility. In other words, you might simply enjoy what you are consuming, or you might find it useful for a practical purpose. Either way, you are actively seeking it out.

In an empowered classroom, this involves allowing students to geek out on their favorite subjects and topics. It involves tapping into *their* interests rather than trying to make things interesting for them.

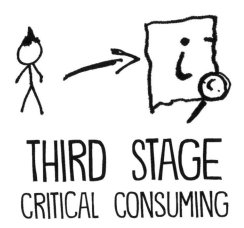

THIRD STAGE
CRITICAL CONSUMING

Here you start to become an expert. You see the nuances in a topic. You begin to appreciate the craft involved in making what you are consuming. You are able to distinguish between good and bad quality.

In an empowered classroom, teachers can provide opportunities for this critical consuming through larger projects, like Genius Hour Projects, Wonder Days, and student choice blogs; however, you can also tap into this critical consuming by allowing students to engage in research or choose their own novels for silent reading.

As their tastes develop, they begin to shift into the next phase of curation.

FOURTH STAGE
CURATING

After becoming an expert, you start picking out the best and commenting on it. You collect things, organize things, and share your reviews with others. In this phase, you are both a fan and a critic.

Curation is actually a vital, lifelong thinking skill. In an age of information saturation, curators are able to seek out the best resources and share them with a unique lens. It is no wonder that some of the most popular blogs in the last few years (*Brain Pickings, Farnam Street, FiveThrityEight*) have been curation blogs that pick apart ideas, data, or published works of others and then share those insights in a unique way.

But it doesn't stop there. As you move through curation, you often find yourself inspired to make something of your own.

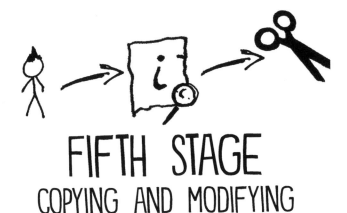

FIFTH STAGE
COPYING AND MODIFYING

This is the part that drives me crazy as a teacher. After developing a level of expertise on a particular work (or artist or style), students will literally copy it. A student who is an amazing artist insists on drawing, line-for-line, a manga or anime work. A student who geeks out on bridges decides she wants to make an exact replica of another bridge. A student gets into food and never deviates from the recipe.

Until … something changes. A student branches out and modifies the copycat work. Suddenly that work becomes a template rather than simply something to copy.

In an empowered classroom, we can help students distinguish between plagiarism and inspiration. We can help them figure out how to use a work as a starting point but then take creative risks and modify what already exists. It's critical that they understand issues around Copyright and Fair Use, but it should be something addressed as a learning experience rather than a punitive measure.

Over time, they start finding inspiration in multiple sources. This, in turn, leads to the next stage.

SIXTH STAGE
MASH-UPS

Sometimes this looks like collage art. Kids combine elements from various favorite works that they have curated, and then make something new. This might not seem all that creative at first glance, but do a simple YouTube search of mash-up songs and you'll get a glimpse into the wildly creative side of the mash-up culture.

Sometimes it looks more like fan fiction. So that student who loved all things Hogwarts-related writes stories about Harry Potter's mother back when she was in Hogwarts. In this way, the things that inspire a student become the imaginative starting place for a new work.

Other times, the mash-up involves taking an idea from one area and applying it to a new context—which can often look incredibly creative. If the mash-up element seems like a "cheat," just remember that all of our great new ideas are a mash-up of the things in life that have inspired us. After all, it's not an accident that your favorite band sounds similar to a few of their favorite bands.

SEVENTH STAGE
CREATING FROM SCRATCH

Note that the previous phases actually involved a great deal of creativity. But this seventh phase is where students are creating something entirely new from scratch.

This is the stage where students start taking the biggest risks and making things that are truly original. While the ideas are often inspired by the previous six stages, this is where a student finds his or her own voice. It's the stage where a student grows in confidence to the extent that her or she is able to take meaningful risks.

Sometimes people skip stages. Someone might go from falling in love with a novel (second stage) to creating fan fiction (sixth stage) without ever copying anything (the fifth stage). On the other hand, I have almost always skipped the mash-up stage, preferring to move from copying a particular style to jumping out and finding my own voice.

This isn't a formula so much as a general trend you will notice as people move on the journey toward creativity.

Visit EmpowerBook.co to get practical resources for empowering our learners. Join the discussion online using the hashtag #empowerbook.

CHAPTER 8

ASSESSMENT SHOULD BE FUN.
NO, REALLY, WE'RE SERIOUS.

THE SHIFT
FROM TAKING AN ASSESSMENT TO ASSESSING YOUR OWN LEARNING

Visit a basketball court or a skate park or a rock climbing gym and you might just miss something happening all around: assessment. The same is true of that group of kids huddled around their devices building a shared world in Minecraft or maneuvering around a kitchen experimenting with a new recipe, or a group of cubers solving a Rubix cube.

Assessment is everywhere.

But it feels invisible because it's less like a noun and more like a verb. In other words, assessment is something we do—not something we give and take.

Nobody stops in the middle of an ollie to fill out a skateboarding test.

The test is built into it. Did you crash, or not? Nobody stops the game of Minecraft to fill out the world-building rubric and then ask about a pattern of performance; however, they are constantly giving each other feedback in the moment and assessing their own progress.

There's nothing wrong with rubrics. After all, a skater might use a scoring rubric in a competition. There's nothing wrong with a test. After all, cubing competitions are all about the timed test. There's nothing wrong with giving a score or using metrics. After all, that same group of Minecrafters will make a video and check to see the page views and likes.

It's not a question about good or bad types of assessments.

ASSESSMENT IS HAPPENING
IN MINECRAFT, AT THE SKATE
PARK, AND EVERYWHERE ELSE
WHERE KIDS ARE ALREADY
OWNING THEIR LEARNING.

ASSESSMENT IS ONLY

AUTHENTIC

IF THE STUDENTS

OWN THE PROCESS.

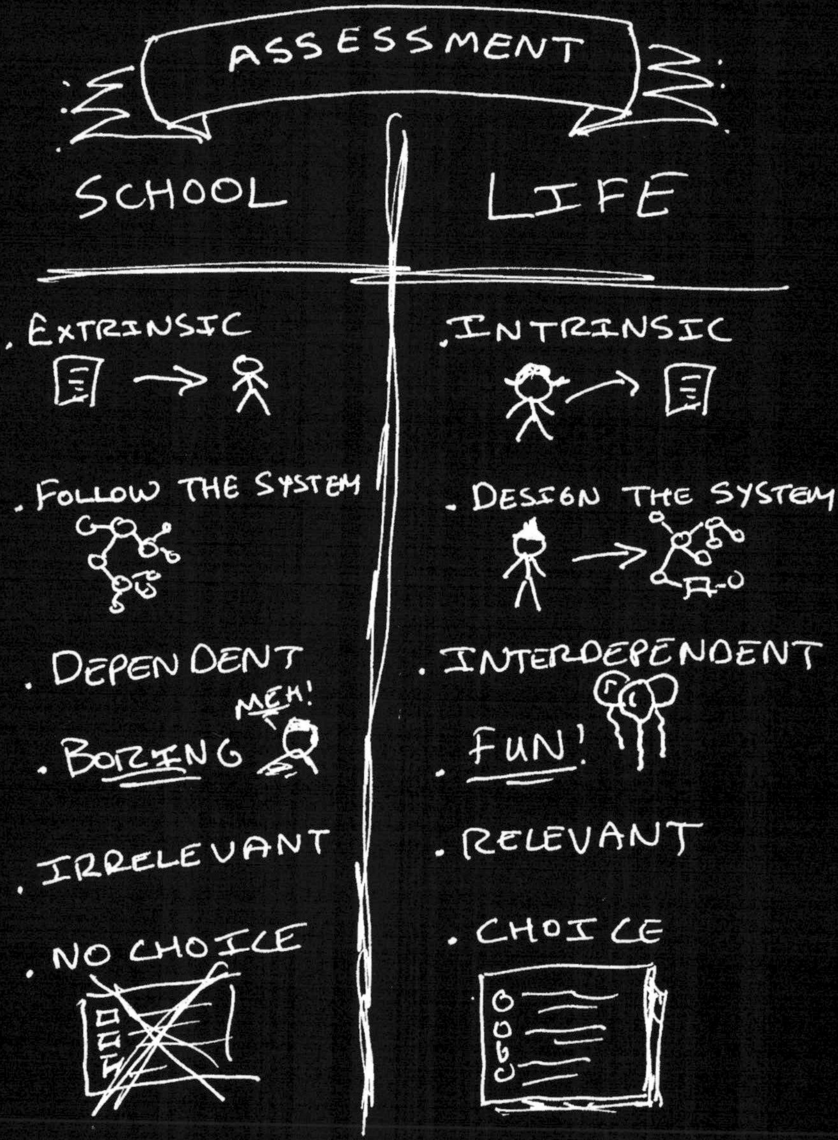
ASSESSMENT
SCHOOL
. EXTRINSIC
. FOLLOW THE SYSTEM
. DEPENDENT
MEH!
. BORING
. IRRELEVANT
. NO CHOICE
LIFE
. INTRINSIC
. DESIGN THE SYSTEM
. INTERDEPENDENT
. FUN!
. RELEVANT
. CHOICE

SO HOW DO WE MAKE ASSESSMENT MORE LIKE LIFE AND LESS LIKE SCHOOL?

The answer lies in student ownership.

When students own the assessment process, they are able to figure out the following:

- What they already know (prior knowledge)

- What they don't know (areas of improvement)

- What they want to master (their goals)

- What they will do to improve (action plan)

Empowered students are able to set goals, monitor their own progress, and determine which types of assessments they will use for specific outcomes. Instead of seeing assessment as a dirty word, they embrace it as a vital part of the learning cycle. It becomes a tool they will use to improve.

WHAT DOES STUDENT OWNERSHIP LOOK LIKE?

This requires a shift from teacher-directed assessment to student-directed assessment; however, this doesn't mean students simply assess their own work at all times. Instead, it involves a collaborative partnership between students, peers, and the teacher. When that happens, students move from being dependent (or independent) and toward interdependence.

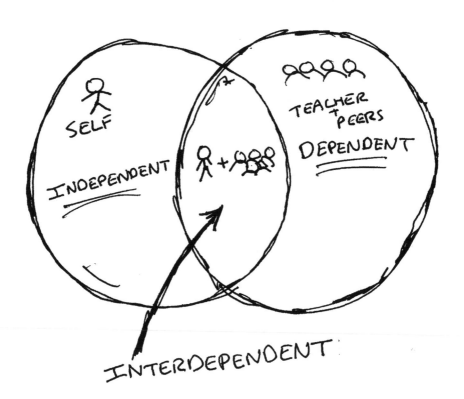

SELF-ASSESSMENT

When students engage in self-assessment, they begin to see their own progress in the moment. They have a more accurate view of their current skill level and a better sense of what they need to do to improve. As they monitor progress and adjust what they are doing, they are able to see the vital role that assessment plays in learning.

But something else happens. They become empowered. Instead of attributing academic success to a teacher or to luck, they see it as a result of their hard work. They grow more self-directed and independent.

This makes sense. Think of the last time you learned a new skill outside of school. Did you wait for a grade? Or did you assess your own progress and make adjustments as a result? Did you feel a sense of awareness about how you were doing and a sense of control over what you needed to do to improve?

The same is true of students.

Let's explore some of the ways students can assess their own learning.

GRAPHING PROGRESS

Students gather their own data and analyze it in a graphical way. It might be a bar graph, a line graph, or a pie chart. The data doesn't have to be from a formal test. It might be something like pages read, words per minute, or tasks finished in a project.

However, the data has to be real and relevant to the students. They need to know what it means and why they are analyzing it. When that happens, those cold, hard numbers begin to feel human.

TRACKING GOALS

Students create their own goals. These can be quantitative or qualitative. Then they keep track of the progress. It might mean a graph, a progress bar, or simply a description of progress.

DATA CAN ACTUALLY BE DEEPLY HUMAN.

HEY! YOU CAN'T ROLL YOUR EYES AT THIS. YOU WERE WARNED BACK IN CHAPTER 1 THAT JOHN WAS A NERD.

SELF-REFLECTIONS

Here students answer reflective questions about what they are learning, where they are struggling, and what they need to do next. Some of the questions might be specific and concrete, while others are broad and abstract.

As they self-reflect, students improve in their metacognition and this, in turn, means they have a better sense of where they are going.

STUDENT SURVEYS

Sometimes students struggle with open-ended self-reflection questions. They can feel too abstract or subjective. Surveys provide a blend of the objective and the subjective.

Students might use a Likert scale, selecting specific words from a bank, or ranking items. This added structure helps students make sense out of something that can feel abstract.

SELF-ASSESSMENT RUBRICS

Students are able to look at the progression from emerging to mastering with specific descriptions in various categories. They are able to gain an accurate view of how they are doing while also having a clear picture of where they need to be.

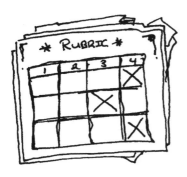

A rubric allows students to think categorically and to see a sense of progression in their work. And when students are assessing their own work with a rubric, they have a greater sense of ownership in the process. They aren't relying on the teacher as the sole source of feedback.

CHECKLISTS

A checklist can be a powerful diagnostic tool that students use before, during, and after a task. Pilots, doctors, and engineers all use checklists as a way to determine whether their work has met specific criteria.

While this might seem simple, it's actually life changing. Sometimes a simple error can lead to disastrous results.

As Atul Gawande points out in Checklist Manifesto: How to Get Things Right,[11]

"One essential characteristic of modern life is that we all depend on systems—on assemblages of people or technologies or both—and among our most profound difficulties is making them work."

When students use checklists, they are learning how to make sense out of systems. They can use a checklist to determine project progress, to assess prototypes, or to make sense out of processes. Or better yet, you can help students create their own checklists based upon criteria you have determined as a class.

PEER ASSESSMENT

Sometimes you miss critical details in self-assessment. You can't see your blind spots because … well … they're your blind spots. In these moments, you need peer feedback to help you see a new perspective.

This idea is built into some of the most innovative companies around.

Take Pixar. They have a brain trust system where people pitch ideas, share their work, and ask for feedback. Everyone in the room has the freedom to criticize. And they do. Often.

This can sound scary; however, it works at Pixar because it is a supportive community. You see, when trust and transparency are present, critical feedback can fuel creative thinking. As Pixar's co-founder Ed Catmull puts it, **"We believe that ideas—and thus, films—only become great when they are challenged and tested."**[12]

Peer feedback is critical for students. Peers are often able to share their thoughts in a more relatable way than teachers.

However, peer assessment can be challenging. We all experience a time crunch. We don't want to burn an entire class period on peer feedback. The second concern is structural. We've all had times when students simply shrug their shoulders and say, "Looks good to me." So here are some structured, shorter ways to provide peer feedback.

BEING HUMBLE
ENOUGH TO ASK
FOR FEEDBACK IS
ACTUALLY A FORM
OF EMPOWERMENT.

THE 10-MINUTE FEEDBACK SYSTEM

This begins with one student sharing their work or pitching an idea while the other student actively listens. It then moves into a chance to ask clarifying questions, get feedback, respond to feedback, and chart out next steps. Each of these stages lasts two to three minutes apiece. While that sounds fast, it can actually feel leisurely because the time is intentional and structured.

Time	Description	Partner A	Partner B
0-2	Elevator Pitch	Describe your idea, plan, or product	Listen
2-4	Clarifying	Answer clarifying questions	Ask clarifying questions
4-6	Feedback	Listen to the feedback without interrupting	Provide specific critical and affirmative feedback
6-8	Paraphrase	Paraphrase what you heard	Listen and clarify
8-10	Next steps	Create next steps	Help guide next steps

STRUCTURED FEEDBACK

Think back to the last time someone gave you great feedback. Chances are it was authentic, specific, and not based upon a rubric or even a checklist. Instead, it was a conversation.

This is the idea of structured feedback. With this type of feedback, you (the teacher) provide specific sentence stems that your students can use to provide diagnostic, clarifying, or critical feedback. This is a powerful way for students to own the assessment process while still having support for their language.

3-2-1 STRUCTURE

This is simple. Students provide three strengths, two areas of improvement, and one question that they have.

THE TEACHER IS STILL VITAL.

While peer feedback and self-assessment are both critical for student ownership, there is value in the kind of feedback students receive from their teachers. Sometimes they need specific feedback from a professional; however we, as teachers, can still empower students during our teacher-initiated assessments. One method is through one-on-one conferencing.

ONE-ON-ONE CONFERENCING

The concept is simple: Plan out three to five mini-conferences per class period. Each conference lasts about five minutes. This generally allows you to meet with each student individually once every two weeks.

Here's a snapshot of one week.

MON	TUES	WED	THURS.	FRI
1	6	11	16	21
2	7	12	17	22
3	8	13	18	23
4	9	14	19	24
5	10	15	20	25

This is where the guide on the side is most powerful.

Students are empowered to ask questions about their work and to reflect on both the product and the process. They are able to navigate how they are doing and what they need to do to improve. Assessment moves from a teacher-directed monologue into a back-and-forth dialogue.

THE THREE TYPES OF CONFERENCES

The following are three types of conferences you can use with students:

#1. Advice Conference: This empowers students to ask for advice. This conference is all about learning specific skills that students are missing. Each student must ask the teacher a series of questions based upon an area where he or she is struggling. This is a chance for targeted one-on-one attention and explicit help with a strategy. Students guide the process, tapping into the teacher's expertise. This has the added bonus of encouraging students to embrace the idea of mistakes as a part of the learning process.

#2. Reflection Conferences: This empowers students to reflect on their learning. Instead of telling students what to do, the goal is to draw out student reflection. The teacher uses a series of reflective questions to lead students through the process of metacognition and into the setting and monitoring of goals. As the year progresses, the teacher asks fewer follow-up questions and the students begin sharing how they are doing without the aid of prechosen questions.

#3 Mastery Conference: Unlike the reflection conference, the focus here is less about reflecting on the process and more about students judging their own mastery of the content.

LET STUDENTS DECIDE

When I (John) first began using self-assessment, peer feedback, and one-on-one conferences, I would choose the structure and require the entire class to use it. Over time, though, I realized that students would use these structures in a more meaningful way if they selected which structure they wanted to use instead.

So I might have a writer's workshop time with some students using the ten-minute peer feedback system while others were using a checklist for self-assessment. It felt chaotic at first, then I realized that they were learning not only how to assess but when to assess, and which type of structure worked best at any given time.

Visit EmpowerBook.co to get practical resources for empowering our learners. Join the discussion online using the hashtag #empowerbook.

CHAPTER 9

OUR LEARNING STORIES MUST INCLUDE FAILING, NOT FAILURE, AND THERE IS A BIG DIFFERENCE BETWEEN THE TWO.

THE SHIFT
FROM FAILURE
TO FAILING

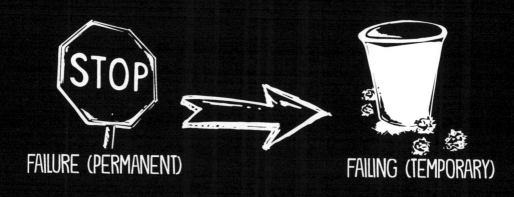

FAILURE (PERMANENT)   FAILING (TEMPORARY)

My (A.J.) daughter lowered her eyes, looked at me, and said, "I can't do it."

I looked back and asked her again to put one foot on the board, push off with her other foot, and then put that foot on the board when she was moving.

She was being a typical six-year-old who was frustrated by trying to learn how to ride a skateboard.

"No," she said, "I'm not doing this anymore. Can you push me?"

It would have been easy for me to help her get both feet on the board and give her a push to get her started. But I had already done that, and now after guiding her through the process (and almost falling myself while demonstrating), it was time for her to keep trying if she wanted to make any progress.

I told her "no" and asked her to try again, this time focusing on getting a good push so she could be moving when she put her foot back on the board.

She was visibly upset. She knew that I could help her out. I knew that I could help her out. But in her mind, she didn't see the bigger picture. She didn't realize that only by trying (and failing) herself would she ever be able to ride a skateboard without my help.

THE PROBLEM WITH THE TERM "FAILURE"

It would be easy to say that this situation is why we need failure in our schools. In real life, we try something, it doesn't work out, we mess up, and we have to keep on moving.

Yet as George Couros, author of *The Innovator's Mindset*, points out on his blog, failure is not necessarily something to be celebrated:

> *I totally understand what educators are saying when they talk about "failure" and our thoughts are on the same wavelength. That being said, the narrative of what teachers actually do is misconstrued by our public when we use the term. Most of the people I know who defend this term do everything in their power to NOT be failures. Since they are educators, that means they do everything to instill "resiliency" and "grit" into their students as well. Do they (or their students) fall? Absolutely. But the story should not be about "falling," it is about what we instill in our students to make sure they get back up. That is what we need to share.*

I know our recent culture of startups and innovation has talked about embracing failure, and I get it.

150

BUT FAIL-URE
HAS A FINALITY TO IT.

FAILURE (PERMANENT)

FAIL-ING IS ALL ABOUT THE PROCESS.

FAILING (TEMPORARY)

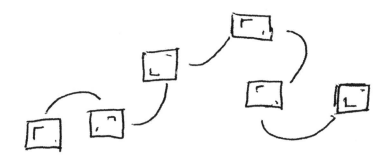

ACTUALLY, WE DON'T WANT STUDENTS TO FAIL. WE WANT THEM TO SUCCEED THROUGH ITERATIONS.

What we really want for our students is not for them to fail, but as Couros points out, for them to get back up and try again. We want them to revise and iterate based on what they learned from failing—all on a path to real success.

When I (A.J.) speak, I often show a video[13] of a skateboarder falling off his board thirty-five times to showcase the difference between fail-ure and fail-ing. He does not give up when he fails. He does not stop trying. Instead, he learns from each mistake and iterates till he gets closer and closer to success.

ALL ABOUT THE FAILING

After we finished our short back-and-forth conversation, my daughter hopped on the skateboard and took off down our driveway. She got both feet on the skateboard and was moving fast. Then, almost like out of a movie, she tried to stop and flew off the back of the board.

I tried to play off the fall by congratulating her.

"Great job getting both feet on the board!"

It didn't help. She was upset and blamed me for the fall (which was partially true). But the next day she was back on the board, this time trying to figure out how to stop.

Learning, it seems, is contagious.

As long as we let students go through the entire process, and we support them along the way as best we can, failing is not a bad thing.

Failure, on the other hand, doesn't include grit, resiliency, and the can-do attitude that make learning contagious.

It's a small change to a powerful word, but I hope it is one we can look at through a learner's eyes.

Here's to failing your way to success, and never adding the "ure" to the end of that word!

Visit EmpowerBook.co to get practical resources for empowering our learners. Join the discussion online using the hashtag #empowerbook.

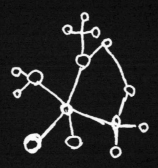

CHAPTER 10

THE SYSTEM SHOULD FIT THE STUDENT INSTEAD OF THE STUDENT FITTING THE SYSTEM.

THE SHIFT
FROM TIERED SYSTEMS TO ADJUSTABLE SYSTEMS

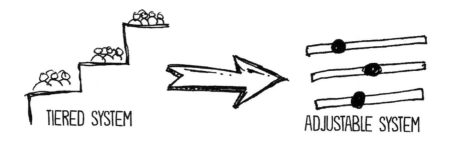

TIERED SYSTEM   ADJUSTABLE SYSTEM

In World War II, the United States faced a high mortality rate in their pilots.[14] They assumed it was an issue of training or of a failure to adjust to faster planes. They continued to explore every possible solution based upon the assumption that there was something inherently wrong with the pilots; however, every tweak they made failed to make a dent in this problem.

Eventually they assessed all of their pilots and concluded that not a one was "average." Out of more than four thousand pilots, they couldn't find a single man who fit the definition of average. Actually few, if any, of the pilots were even close in measurement to the "average man." Average was an illusion meant to make large amounts of messy data seem simpler. It was a human invention that society had accepted as a scientific and mathematical truth.

This revelation shocked the military.

It turned out that the problem wasn't with the pilots, the aircraft, or even the training they had received. The real issue was that they were trying to fit diverse body types into a one-size-fits-all cockpit.

They had to find a new approach. Would they design custom-made cockpits? If so, how would they afford that? What would that mean when pilots retired or died? Was the plane suddenly to become useless?

There were other ideas. Perhaps they would have to choose only the pilots whose body type fit perfectly into one type of cockpit. Again, this was unrealistic, because they needed the most qualified pilots to fight in the war.

Finally they landed on a solution.

MAKE THINGS ADJUSTABLE.

That was it.

Make the helmet straps adjustable. Make the pedals adjustable. Make the seats adjustable. Suddenly the mortality rates plummeted as they embraced this idea of flexible design and quit assuming that people needed to conform to a mythical idea of average.

Instead of trying to fit people into the system, they designed flexibility into their systems. It worked. To this day, pilots still have the freedom to adjust their cockpit to fit their individual needs.

The original system was built on the concept of average. Averages aren't useless; however, they are often used to design systems and structures that are applied to all people (which was the case with the pilots). Worse still, people use averages to try to assess the knowledge, skills, and abilities of individuals. This happens all the time in schools.

You can find the entire story in Todd Rose's TED Talk, "The Myth of Average."

EVERYTHING IS AVERAGE?

Schools are immersed in a system of averaging. We average out the scores on all assignments in order to produce a grade. We use the bell curve to average out student performance and set a curve. How often have you sat in a meeting with charts and graphs of standardized test scores telling you who needs intervention? It is a critical part of everything from RTI to PLCs to any other acronym program that's popular in K–12 education.

But the concept of average is often even more subtle for classroom teachers.

What should the average student know? How long would it take the average student to learn this? How much work should the average student do on this project?

But here's the problem: We don't teach average students.

NONE OF YOUR STUDENTS ARE AVERAGE.

(NONE OF THEM)

There is no such thing as an average student—just as there are no average pilots; however, when we aim for average, we find that the instruction isn't fitting anyone.

Take something as simple as timing. You give students fifteen minutes for a task. Some kids are moving ahead. Others are behind. In this moment, "average" isn't working for anyone. Students are bored, angry, frustrated, and disengaged.

WHY DIFFERENTIATION HAS FAILED US

For years, we have known that students aren't identical. We have watched certain students move full-sprint ahead while others are left behind. As a result, we have embraced a system of differentiation based upon tiered levels.

Here teachers design a different set of instructions for various levels of students. You create three separate sets of problems in math. You have four leveled reading groups for literature circles. You create a hard, medium, and easy versions of the writing assignment.

TIERED SYSTEM

While differentiation is a step in the right direction, it often fails to meet individual needs; for example, that student who is in the "low" reading group might struggle with comprehension but is amazing at making inferences. That student taking on the low-level algebra problems might understand linear relationships at a deep level but struggle with computational fluency.

But it's more than just skill level. We also know that each student has a different set of interests and passions and prior knowledge. Each student has a different set of questions. Each student has a different system that works for them.

So where does that leave us? Are we supposed to design thirty-two separate lesson plans each day?

There is a different option.

BUT FIRST, LET'S TALK ABOUT ICE CREAM.

THAT'S RIGHT.
ICE CREAM.

YEP.
ICE CREAM.

Baskin Robbins offers thirty-one flavors. The rotation changes each month, so I'm guessing there are probably hundreds if not thousands of flavors that they create. If you're looking for choice, this place is it. And there's a good chance you'll find something that you like at the store. If you can't find something you like, you might want to reconsider your life ... or at least your love of ice cream.

However, if you are looking for something very specific that nobody in their right mind would offer, you might need to go to Cold Stone Creamery. Here you can order a hot-fudge-peanut-butter-and-pretzel ice cream. Nobody else is choosing that flavor. It's yours. There's a good chance you'll get the exact ice cream that you want.

And yet ...

If you want to own the entire process, you need to go to a frozen yogurt place. I know, I know, it's not really ice cream. It's "yogurt," which is a code word for "ice cream that pretends not to be ice cream."

At the fro-yo place, you get to decide which flavor you want. There are fewer options than what Baskin Robbins offers; however, you get to decide on the exact amount you want. You also get to choose the toppings, selecting not only which ones you want but how much you want of each topping.

You own the entire process.

GOING BEYOND DIFFERENTIATION

When we talk about choice and differentiation, the conversations often revolve around the Baskin Robbins model. The "lower level" groups get one scoop, and the advanced students get three scoops.

Or it's about specific choices. Give them a choice menu and let them decide on the flavor. On some level, it works. As the teacher, you get to do quality control on the content and on the process. But it can feel exhausting to create thirty-one new flavors over and over again.

Sometimes we shift from differentiated to personalized. This is when the Cold Stone Creamery model kicks in. Here students move from choice to freedom in the content. They are not selecting from a list of choices, rather they are stating exactly what they want. There is more ownership. Engagement increases, but the teacher still owns the process and it becomes exhausting.

When students own both the content and the process, they shift into the fro-yo model. Here they decide what they want to learn by doing it themselves. They select the exact amount of yogurt they need and they focus on toppings they think are both interesting and necessary. The teacher is still present as an advisor and an architect of the master system; however, students are working in a self-directed way.

If Baskin Robbins is differentiation and Cold Stone Creamery is personalization, frozen yogurt is empowerment based upon a system of flexible design.

THERE IS NOTHING WRONG WITH ANY OF THESE MODELS.

There are times when the entire class needs to work together, and there are very few options present. They might be engaging in a debate or analyzing an article, and the lack of choice is precisely what keeps the community unified.

There are moments when you shift into a Baskin Robbins model and use choice menus or set up leveled systems. There's nothing wrong with this. Sometimes you need small groups at different reading levels or you need specific choice options for math problems.

There are times when you move into personalization. It takes extra work on your part, but it's worth it in the long run. You are meeting with students one-on-one and conferencing or tutoring. You are finding specific things to engage specific students.

However, there is also a time for a frozen yogurt mindset. Here you allow students to own the process and the product. They are self-directed, choosing the topic, the themes, the product, the ideas, and the questions based upon their own desires, passions, curiosity, and mastery. They are selecting the intervention and enrichment.

EMBRACING FLEXIBLE DESIGN

In the earlier story, the military assumed that their pilots were incompetent or poorly trained. They blamed the pilots instead of the system; however, when they shifted away from fitting the pilots into their design and started adapting their design to fit the individual pilots, everything changed.

But they didn't do this by designing custom seats for every pilot. Instead, they created flexible options and let the pilots customize it according to their needs.

You might expect to have a short, medium, and tall version of a seat in a plane. Instead, they made the seat adjustable and let each pilot chose the setting that worked best for him. The first approach depends on averaging and differentiating. It is what we do in schools when we group students and then use tracking for differentiation. But this second idea is different. It keeps things flexible and allows the user to make the decision about differentiation.

What if our lessons, projects, units, and assignments were adjustable? What if our rules, procedures, and structures were flexible? What if students felt the permission to modify things on their own? What if we adapted the system for the students rather than forcing the students to fit into the system?

In other words, we can make it less like Baskin Robbins and more like frozen yogurt.

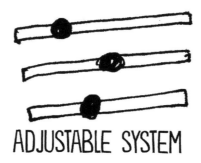

ADJUSTABLE SYSTEM

As we design adjustable systems, it can help to ask, "How can this be more adjustable? What can students do to modify this to meet their own needs?"

CREATE LOOSELY STRUCTURED PROJECTS.

You can create loosely structured projects where students have more autonomy in what they are creating and how they are making it.

This also means getting rid of specific numbers on assignments (three pages, five paragraphs, etc.) and allowing students to determine the quantity on their own. Students can also choose the format for their projects and integrate multimedia where they see fit.

SELECT THE SKILLS, STRATEGIES, AND STANDARDS.

Encourage students to self-select the skills they are practicing. So instead of continuing to re-learn things they already know, they have extended time to practice in areas where they are struggling.

Help students learn how to select which particular strategies work best for their own learning.

This approach can feel nerve-wracking, both for the students and for the teacher. It's why it can help to move incrementally toward more student choice and flexible design.

This approach also requires a deep sense of trust from the teacher. It can be hard to say, "Go ahead and modify this to fit your needs."

Sometimes students will need additional help. Certain students who struggle with executive functioning might need additional directions or structures to help them determine what to do. But even then, they're getting the chance to maneuver their way around a flexible system.

When students feel empowered, they begin to own their learning in a way unimaginable before.

OKAY, BUT WHAT DOES THIS LOOK LIKE?

Imagine you're a fifth-grade student in a language arts block. Instead of leveled reading groups followed by writing prompts, you are given the chance to create a blog.

You choose the topic.

You choose the theme.

In this case, you're going for a video game blog. You then spend a good part of the class period pursuing a question about gaming and reading through several articles. Based upon a one-on-one conference with your teacher, you know that you struggle with clarifying questions, so you select that as your standard on which you will focus as you research.

You go to the online tutorials whenever you feel lost on this process. But you also talk to a peer and share your expertise in making inferences. She double-checks your clarifying questions. The intervention is built into the process.

It's not 100 percent individualized. After all, the entire class is focused on citing evidence in their writing, so there are a few short mini-lessons on how to fact-check articles and find relevant information. Still, you own this research process. You are the pilot, and you are customizing the cockpit to fit your needs.

Eventually you move into writing your blog post. You end up with a sprawling five-paragraph piece. The person next to you has one introduction and a short list. The person across from you just finished a podcast.

Nobody is on the same page.

It's a bit of a mess.

But it doesn't matter.

It's frozen yogurt. Every work is supposed to be different.

Visit EmpowerBook.co to get practical resources for empowering our learners. Join the discussion online using the hashtag #empowerbook.

CHAPTER 11

STORIES ARE EMPOWERING
IF WE OWN THEM.

You may have missed it along the way, but your class has a story. You might have been caught up in the everyday grind, or you were overwhelmed or possibly just enjoying the moment ... but your class and your school has a story.

We eat, live, and learn with our students for almost ten months. We watch them fail. We watch them grow. We see them connect and collaborate. We help them create and build. Yet as the school year comes to a close, it's time to look at your class story. Because every class is different, and every story has a different ending.

Empowered students are those who see their story continue beyond the walls and doors of our schools, beyond the seven-hour days, and beyond the final bell.

Empowered students craft their own learning stories and relish the opportunity to add to this story while in school, not waiting for graduation to do something impactful.

WHO IS THE HERO OF YOUR CLASSROOM STORY?

HOW TO TELL A STORY

I (A.J.) recently read Donald Miller's book *How to Tell a Story*.[15] It was a quick read, but one that caught me a bit off guard. Sometimes we take stories for granted or think that they are "just for kids," but as adults, we shape our lives through stories. Each day has a beginning, middle, and end. Each life situation, each job, and each year is shaped in much the same way.

The same goes for your class and the school year. Miller gives a simple story structure that is used in thousands of books, movies, and in our own lives. Here's a sketch-note version of the idea:

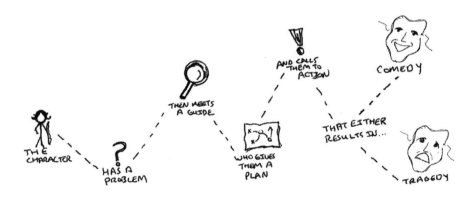

Let's look at how this applies to your class.

The character in your class story could be an individual student or the entire class. Once you've defined the character, the next step is understanding what the problem is/was.

MY CLASS STORY

I (A.J.) have written a lot about the 20% Time project in my class a few years ago. Using the previous visual, let's think through the class story. The characters (my students) had a problem (they were solely focused on what grade they received and not the learning experience).

They met a guide (me) who gave them a plan (the 20% Time project). I called them to action: Learn what you want and what you are passionate about—and not because I'm giving you a grade. That ended in a success (happy ending when the presentations came through with amazing work that was not tied to grades).

That's the whole group story.

But inside this class story would be many individual stories. One such story could look like this: The character (a girl in my class) had a problem (she was afraid to share her own music with the world). She met a guide (a mentor we found through the project) who gave her a plan (she didn't need to perform in front of people at first) and called her to action (she was to record herself and put it up online anonymously and write about it), that ended in a success (she received positive feedback online and eventually added her name and more songs).

YOU ARE THE GUIDE.

The point is to view your class and each individual student as a story waiting to happen …

Okay, but if students are on this epic adventure, and they are taking charge of their own learning, what does that mean for the teacher?

As a teacher, we are often the guide who calls the character (class or student) to action; however, we can also sometimes point the character to a different guide (it doesn't always have to be us) who may be able to help better for various circumstances.

This can feel humbling. And it is. When you move toward being a guide, you are giving up power and control. Students are making more decisions. They own both the individual and collective story. Being a "guide" can feel like you now occupy a diminished role.

SO DOES BEING A "GUIDE ON THE SIDE" MEAN YOU LOSE YOUR INFLUENCE?

THE SHORT ANSWER IS "NO."

GUIDES ARE ACTUALLY PRETTY INFLUENTIAL.

Think of these magical guides from epic stories:

GANDALF   YODA   MS. FRIZZLE

Does anyone doubt their awesomeness? Especially Ms. Frizzle, who beats out Gandalf as a teacher because he's been known to say, "You shall not pass," while the Frizz makes sure everyone is learning. Okay, so maybe Gandalf was actually stopping a demon.

But each of these guides played a powerful role by building relationships and bringing out the heroes in others.

Joseph Campbell[16] coined the term "hero's journey" to describe the structure of epic stories. Here the hero is called into a difficult concept but emerges at the end a changed person.

Notice that the guide plays a huge role here:

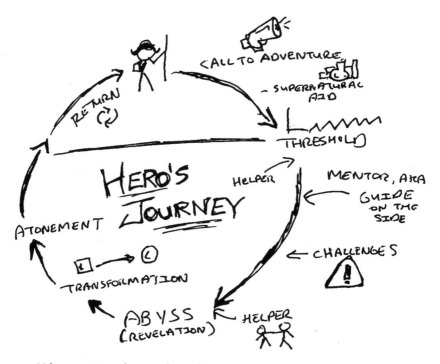

(Also notice that John's handwriting is almost illegible.)

EVERY PROJECT IS A STORY.

While the school year is a larger epic (maybe an epic series), every project has the potential to also be an epic story where the students are heroes tackling meaningful problems and finding the themes in the process.

STORY ELEMENT	PROJECT ELEMENT
PROTAGONIST	STUDENT, WHO DIRECTS THE STORY
THE GUIDE	TEACHER, WHO MENTORS STUDENTS
CONFLICT	PROBLEM THAT STUDENTS CARE ABOUT
THEME	MEANINGFUL LESSONS THAT EMERGE
SETTING	AUTHENTIC CONTEXT
INCITING INCIDENT	STARTING PLACE OFF INQUIRY
CLIMAX	STUDENTS CREATE, SOLVE, LAUNCH
RESOLUTION	STUDENTS ARE EMPOWERED

CRAFTING YOUR CLASS STORY

Teaching is not always easy. And learning can be a struggle for many of our students. As educators, we are called to this back-and-forth process of teaching and learning. We push and challenge, and then support and guide. It's easy to get lost in the grind. It's why so many teachers get burnt out … and why so many students complain about school.

However, if we think about each school year as a journey—one that will not only come to an end but also lead to new journeys—then our mindset changes from dealing with the grind to crafting the best story possible.

When talking to students at the beginning of the year (or throughout the course), make sure they understand the journey you are about to take, because as Miller points out, people understand complicated concepts when presented in story format.

If you want people to understand and identify with a complicated concept, tell a story about it.

Telling a story often creates a "clicking experience" in a person's brain, allowing them to suddenly understand what someone else is trying to say. As such, those who can tell good stories will create faster, stronger connections with others.

ACTUALLY, YOU'RE MORE THAN JUST A GUIDE ON THE SIDE.

There is a popular phrase in education that teachers must be a "guide on the side" instead of the "sage on the stage." The thought is that we should be facilitating the learning from the side instead of preaching to students about what they should learn.

But that's not entirely accurate. Here's the piece that many teachers (myself included) often miss.

Sometimes the main character in the story isn't the student. Sometimes the main character is the teacher.

I can't tell you how many times I've gone through a school year and had my students guide me and call me to action.

We're all a part of the epic adventure. We're all learning from one another.

In fact, the best stories occur when I'm joining them on the adventure, when we are embarking together and learning by each other's side. We may be learning different lessons along the way, but the journey is shared.

If we look at our students' learning stories as shared journeys in which we take an active role, then we are more than guides on the side.

WE ARE GUIDES ON THE RIDE.

We are active participants in this adventure, and we learn just as much as our students do throughout the process.

When students are empowered to craft their own learning stories and go on shared learning journeys, they'll often take the chance to dramatically impact their own lives (and the lives of others) through what they make, create, design, and explore.

Visit EmpowerBook.co to get practical resources for empowering our learners. Join the discussion online using the hashtag #empowerbook.

CHAPTER 12

THE STARTING POINT FOR
EMPOWERING YOUR STUDENTS

#1: START WITH ONE PROJECT.

Student ownership is a big idea. It takes time to develop the systems and structures for things like student-selected intervention, enrichment, and student self-assessments. Besides, you probably have great lessons that aren't necessarily choice driven (like that amazing read-aloud with that Socratic Seminar built into it).

This is the start of a journey. It will take years to figure out what works for you. But that's okay. Every small act of student ownership is another step in the journey.

Sometimes it helps to start out with one choice-driven project. This allows you to spend some time planning and reflecting while also continuing to teach in a way that feels comfortable. It might be a two-week unit that you try out. Or it might be a day-long project that you can try on a "wasted day" like the day before Spring Break or the last day of state mandated testing.

In the next few pages, we'll be exploring some of the projects you can use as a starting point to student choice.

WONDER WEEK

The Wonder Week Project is an inquiry-based, week-long project where students ask questions about anything they find interesting. These are those nagging questions they have that they've never had a chance to answer in school.

NEVER FORGET TO EMBRACE WONDER.

GENIUS HOUR

If you want to go fully independent and long term, you can try a Genius Hour Project. Here students spend an allotted time each week working independently on a project that they design from the ground up.

Genius Hour is an innovative approach to choice, inspired by Google's 20% Time that they offer employees. The idea is that one day a week, employees at Google get to work on passion projects. These independent projects have led to some of the best innovations that Google has seen.

This might be hard to pull off in a classroom, but it's possible.

Students can plan and manage their own independent projects. Some students will work alone, while others work collaboratively. Some of the projects begin with questions and research, while others start with students learning how to do something creative for the first time. It's meant to be flexible.

GEEK OUT BLOGS

The idea is simple. Students write topical or thematic blogs on the topics that they geek out about. We go over examples of blogs (which exposes students to high-interest non-fiction reading) and they look at trends. They see foodie blogs, skateboarding blogs, sports blogs, fashion blogs, gaming blogs, car blogs, history blogs, science blogs, etc.

Next they create a specifically themed blog. They define the driving interest as well as the audience. From there they begin writing blog posts in various formats:

1. They choose the format, including video, audio, and text.

2. They choose the topics of the posts.

3. They engage in research and share their findings with the classmates.

4. They create posts that range from listicles to Q&A to interviews to human interest stories to persuasive pieces to instructions on how to do something.

With Geek Out Blogs, students get to own the entire writing process from finding a topic and an audience all the way into research, writing, editing, and publishing. They get to choose the format and the genre of each post. And ultimately, they get to be the experts.

#2: COLLABORATE WITH A TRUSTED COLLEAGUE.

When I first started shifting toward a choice-driven classroom, I felt alone. I became risk-averse because I didn't want to look like the "odd one out." I made huge mistakes, and I had no one with whom to share my frustrations because I knew I would hear things like,

- You were too idealistic.
- Maybe kids shouldn't have so much choice in their learning.
- Too much choice will make kids selfish.

However, in my second year in this shift, I met a new teacher named Javier. He and I became close friends and trusted colleagues. We regularly shared what worked and what failed. We were able to be vulnerable. And slowly we started collaborating on projects. It was easier to take creative risks when I wasn't alone.

#3: DO A CHOICE AUDIT OF YOUR CLASSROOM.

It can help to do an audit of every classroom procedure with the driving question, "What am I doing for students that they could do on their own?" This not only empowers students but also frees up the teacher to spend less time working as a mid-level manager and more time as an instructional leader.

It can help to close your eyes and imagine yourself as a student. Go through the entire class period or school day in your classroom and imagine what you, as a student, would want to do on your own.

This sense of empathy can be eye-opening. When I did this, I realized that most of the class procedures had been designed to make things easier for me as the teacher. They weren't oriented around students; however, when students owned more of the process, things actually became more organized and less chaotic because students weren't having to figure out how to comply with an external system.

Ask yourself what systems you currently have that could be redesigned as flexible systems.

#4: RETHINK THE STANDARDS.

Chances are you have a set of standards and a curriculum map that corresponds to it. You might even have a specific curriculum you have to follow.

It can help to view standards as the structure for choice. It's more like a blueprint; however, you get to build it, decorate it, and make it yours.

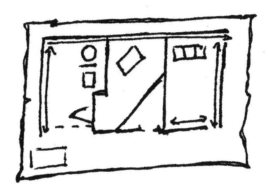

Look at the standards and ask the following:

1. What part of this standard is content-neutral? Is it possible for students to select themes or topics?

2. What part of this could be tied to other standards? Can we chunk them and layer them?

3. What choices can students make when using this standard?

4. How can students self-select strategies connected to this standard?

#5: COMMUNICATE WITH STAKEHOLDERS.

(Not to be confused with steak holders,
which is totally different.)

Sometimes student choice can seem like negligence to parents or principals. You can appear as the "fun teacher" who is "letting kids get away with everything."

It can be helpful to share your vision with your administrators, colleagues, and students' parents. Share data with parents about how student choice could increase motivation and engagement. Help people to understand that this isn't simply an issue of letting kids do whatever they feel like doing.

Let your administrator know that you will still have structures, rules, and expectations. Use the word "pilot" to describe things like design thinking and/or inquiry-based learning.

Seriously.

Go try it out.

Leaders love it.

Say something like, "I'm going to pilot Genius Hour Projects." Or say, "We will be piloting the use of design thinking, a framework used in the arts, business, and engineering." Share that with your administrators and with your parents. Chances are they'll see choice as more than just letting go and having fun.

#6: MODEL IT.

Students aren't always used to the sheer amount of choice you're providing. You may need to teach students how to select the right intervention and enrichment, how to access the scaffolding, how to manage their own projects, and how to make decisions when they feel stuck.

It helps to take a gradual-release approach. When you're learning a skill for the first time, chances are you watch tons of videos. You copy other people. You listen to experts. You are risk averse. You wonder if you're doing it right.

The same is true of students who are owning their learning for the first time. They need a vision for how it can look, and you, as the teacher, can provide that to them by modeling. Sometimes you will have to give permission when you assume they already know it. Sometimes you will have to model the metacognition needed in self-assessment. Sometimes you need to model the decision-making process. It's okay if there's some direct instruction in these early stages of student choice. Students need to see what it looks like in action.

#7: TAKE THE LEAP!

It won't be easy. It won't be perfect. You'll make mistakes. But it's an epic adventure.

EMPOWER

WHY STUDENT OWNERSHIP MATTERS

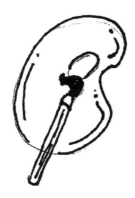

THE MURAL PROJECT

It was a simple idea. Three girls noticed that every time we painted over graffiti at our school, the tagging reappeared within twenty-four hours. They said it made them feel unsafe and nervous and they wanted to fix this problem in their community. At first, they looked into raising money for a camera system or maybe organizing a neighborhood watch organization.

But as they researched it, a trend emerged. Many of the taggers viewed themselves as graffiti artists canvassing boring industrial spaces with their names. These weren't gang-related threats. **These were people wanting to be known.** This didn't excuse the vandalism, but it changed the girls' perceptions of it.

This led to a **bold** idea.

One of the girls approached me (John) with a two-page plan. I didn't get a chance to read it before she blurted out the idea: "We'll cover it with art. We think that the taggers will leave the art alone."

"Like an art gallery?"

"No, murals. We'll have murals everywhere."

She then launched into a five-minute explanation of what our campus would look like when they were finished. We pitched the idea to our principal, who gave us the green light immediately.

This was the start of a massive project. Small groups met in teams to plan out everything from materials to processes to the overall design concept. We landed on the idea of immigration and the reminder that we are a patchwork of cultures. This one boy, Michael, sketched out the entire concept, and we used the grid system to scale it onto the wall.

THEY OWNED THE PROCESS.

We spent a week sketching out the design. Five students before school. Seven students after school. On that first Saturday, twelve groggy-eyed students met me at sun up on a cool desert morning to paint it. Suddenly the vision of a mural became a reality as students busted out the paint brushes and transformed the white wall into a work of art.

It wasn't perfect. We made so many mistakes. We had moments where students stormed off in frustration. But we continued on with the project with our two rules:

1. MISTAKES ARE ALLOWED. IT'S HOW WE LEARN.

2. EVERYONE IS AN ARTIST, SO EVERYONE GETS A VOICE.

After four hours, we had a solid start. But after cleaning up the painting mess, I drove away wondering if this would be covered up with graffiti by Monday morning. This was risky.

Nobody touched the mural. They continued to tag up the rest of the school, but the mural had a sort-of force field of creativity and student voice around it. We spent two months painting the mural and accidentally painting part of the sidewalk (we didn't think to use a drop cloth).

Nobody touched it.

For an entire summer, the mural remained as a bold statement of unity for the entire neighborhood to see. The next year, we painted two more murals.

What began as a project grew into a movement.

In three years, we painted five murals. It was a source of pride. I would watch little kids walking to the nearby elementary school stop in their tracks and point and stare.

Moms would say to their kids, "Someday you'll get to paint one."

But at the close of our third year, we had a change in leadership and suddenly everything changed. We showed up after Spring Break and the walls were white. The official reason was that these murals looked "unprofessional" and we needed a "fresh start" as the school shifted from a middle school into a K–8.

"Why did we even bother?" a boy asked me as he fought back tears.

"Maybe we could …"

"No, Mr. Spencer. I'm not painting anything else. I'm moving my blog to private. You never know when the haters are going to show up. I'm done sharing my work."

I looked him in the eyes and said,

"WHEN YOU HIDE YOUR VOICE FROM THE WORLD, YOU ROB THE WORLD OF YOUR CREATIVITY. I'M NOT GOING TO LET YOU GET AWAY WITH THAT."

That afternoon as I drove home, it struck me that I had echoed the same words Mrs. Smoot had said to me back when I was in the eighth grade.

And I realized that the real power in the mural project was the power of empowering students. They were different because they had owned the learning.

Projects come and go. Technology changes. Ideas go in and out of style. And, yes, people paint over murals. All art is, on some level, temporary. But there's something you can't take away, and it's the mindset that students develop when they define themselves as makers. When that happens, lives are changed. The world is different, and their world is better.

Visit EmpowerBook.co to get practical resources for empowering our learners. Join the discussion online using the hashtag #empowerbook.

YOUR INVITATION TO INNOVATION

THIS IS YOUR INVITATION TO ...

☐ REWRITE THE RULES

☐ CHALLENGE THE STATUS QUO

☐ LET YOUR STUDENTS OWN THEIR LEARNING

☐ CHANGE THE WORLD

NOTES

1: Page viii
Couros, G. (2015, August 18). "Hard Work is No Guarantee of Success." Retrieved May 26, 2017, from georgecouros.ca/blog/archives/5494.

2: Page ix
A quote by Steve Jobs. (n.d.). Retrieved May 26, 2017, from goodreads.com/quotes/936174-because-the-people-who-are-crazyenough-to-think-they.

3: Page xix
Average hours spent in school per day in the United States as reported by the National Center for Education Statistics: nces.ed.gov/surveys/sass/tables/sass0708_035_s1s.asp.

Schools and Staffing Survey (SASS). (n.d.). Retrieved May 26, 2017, from nces.ed.gov/surveys/sass/tables/sass0708_035_s1s.asp.

4: Page xxiv
Friedman, T. L. "How to Get a Job at Google." *New York Times*. February 22, 2014. Retrieved May 26, 2017, from nytimes.com/2014/02/23/opinion/sunday/friedman-how-to-get-a-job-at-google.html.

5: Page xxix
Bill Ferriter's article explaining difference between engagement and empowerment: Ferriter, W. (2014, January 28). "Should We Be Engaging OR Empowering Learners?" Retrieved May 26, 2017, from blog.williamferriter.com/2014/01/28/should-we-be-engaging-or-empowering-learners.

6: Page xxx
Phil Schlechty's Levels of Engagement as shared through the Schlechty Center: Schlechty, P. (n.d.). Tools. Retrieved May 26, 2017, from schlechtycenter.org/tools/.

7: Page 12
The Story of Louis Braille: Louis Braille. (n.d.) (2017, May 22). In Wikipedia. Retrieved May 26, 2017, from en.wikipedia.org/wiki/Louis_Braille.

8:Page 19
"The Toffler Legacy," Toffler Associates, tofflerassociates.com/about/the-toffler-legacy/?fa=galleryquotes.

9: Page 37
National survey on students stressed out and bored. The survey, called Emotion Revolution, is a joint effort between the Yale Center for Emotional Intelligence and the Born This Way Foundation, referenced in this article: "Students Unhappy in School, Survey Finds," *Inside Health News*. (n.d.).

Retrieved May 26, 2017, from blogs.webmd.com/breaking-news/2015/10/students-unhappy-in-school-survey-finds.html.

10: Page 43
Dale Carnegie quote from his wildly popular book (which we recommend) titled, *How to Win Friends and Influence People*. (n.d.) (2017, May 25). In Wikipedia. Retrieved May 26, 2017, from en.wikipedia.org/wiki/How_to_Win_Friends_and_Influence_People.

11: Page 138
Gawande, Atul, *The Checklist Manifesto: How to Get Things Right* (New York, NY: Henry Holt, 2011) pg. 184.

12: Page 154
Amazing commitment and persistence video of skateboarder shared on Michael Babich YouTube Channel: youtube.com/watch?v=zVrtp3rUS3s&feature=youtu.be.

Amazing commitment and persistence. (2015, October 19). Retrieved May 26, 2017, from youtube.com/watch?v=zVrtp3rUS3s&feature=youtu.be.

13: page 139
Catmull, Ed. *Creativity, Inc.* New York: Random House, 2014.

14: Page 159
Learn more about "the myth of average" from Todd Rose in his book *The End of Average* and his TEDx Talk on the subject: toddrose.com/endofaverage/T. (2013, June 19). "The Myth of Average: Todd Rose at TEDxSonomaCounty." Retrieved May 26, 2017, from youtube.com/watch?v=4eBmyttcfU4.

15: Page 180
Check out Donald Miller's free eBook, *How to Tell a Story*, and more resources on the power of story on his website: storylineblog.com/how-to-tell-a-story/Miller, D. (n.d.). Scary Close. Retrieved May 26, 2017, from storylineblog.com/how-to-tell-a-story/.

16: Page 184
Joseph Campbell's "The Hero's Journey" inspired us as teachers and is still relevant today. Learn about it here: en.wikipedia.org/wiki/The_Hero%27s_Journey_(book). Hero's journey. (n.d.) (2017, May 24). In Wikipedia. Retrieved May 26, 2017, from en.wikipedia.org/wiki/Hero%27s_journey.

ABOUT THE AUTHORS

JOHN SPENCER

John Spencer is on a quest to see teachers transform their spaces into bastions of creativity and wonder and to empower students to develop a maker mindset through design thinking. After spending twelve years as an urban middle school teacher, Spencer is now a full-time professor of educational technology and a leader in creativity, design thinking, and student-centered learning. He is the co-founder of two educational startups and the co-author of a top-selling children's book.

As a dad, he loves to make stuff with his children, whether it involves writing comics, building a model roller coaster with recycled material, or making a city with LEGOS (which are awesome until you step on them at four in the morning).

John shares his vision for creative classrooms through his blog (spencerauthor.com) and his illustrated videos (spencervideos.com). You can connect with him on Twitter (@spencerideas) or on his Facebook page (facebook.com/spencereducation/).

BRING JOHN SPENCER TO YOUR SCHOOL OR EVENT

John Spencer is passionate about seeing educators embrace design thinking and creativity. Over the last few years, he has shared this vision for creative classroom with a variety of audiences, including his speech in the White House about the future of education and his TEDx Talk on creativity.

John offers a creative, thought-provoking, and humorous style through his keynotes, full-day workshops, and online professional development.

He offers the unique perspective of being a published author, the co-founder of a successful startup, an award-winning classroom teacher, and a college professor. He uses this blend of classroom experience, industry experience, and research experience to craft innovative, holistic, and practical learning experiences in a style that is approachable and relevant.

WHAT PEOPLE ARE SAYING ABOUT JOHN SPENCER

"John's classroom and research expertise on project-based learning, design thinking, and blended literacy allows him to offer realistic and practical suggestions to move teachers forward. John's amazing creativity can be seen in his humor, writing, drawings, and engaging presentation style."

"John Spencer is a fantastic speaker. He will inspire you and push your thinking to new heights. His mixture of content, storytelling, and humor makes for a great keynote."

"John inspires and empowers. I rarely say that something transforms my practice, but this design-thinking workshop changed the way I teach."

POPULAR MESSAGES FROM JOHN SPENCER

John often speaks on creativity, design thinking, student-centered pedagogy, project-based learning, and meaningful technology integration. His workshops and keynotes are tailored specifically with your audience and include a set of resources customized for your context. Here are a few of his most recent examples:

1. The Future of Learning: Redefining Relevance in a Creative Age

2. Empowered: Making the Shift from Engagement to Ownership

3. The Creative Classroom: Boosting Creativity and Innovation through Design Thinking

4. The Seven Types of Creative Teachers

5. Epic Learning: Lesson Planning through the Lens of Story

CONNECT

Connect with John Spencer for more information about bringing him to your event.

Email: john@spencerauthor.com

Twitter: @spencerideas

Blog: spencerauthor.com

YouTube: spencervideos.com and videoprompts.com

A.J. JULIANI

A.J. Juliani is the director of technology and innovation at Centennial School District and a leading educator in the area of innovation, design thinking, and inquiry-based learning. Juliani has worked as a middle and high school English teacher, a K–12 technology staff developer, and an education and technology innovation specialist.

A.J. is the author of books centered around student agency, choice, innovative learning, and empowerment. As a parent of four young children, A.J. believes we must be intentional about innovation in order to create a better future of learning for all of our students. You can connect with A.J. on his blog, "Intentional Innovation" (located at ajjuliani.com) or through Twitter (@ajjuliani).

BRING A.J. JULIANI TO YOUR SCHOOL OR EVENT

A.J. Juliani brings a high-energy, fun, and engaging style of presentation through keynotes, full-day workshops, and online professional development offerings. His mix of personal stories from the classroom, real-world examples, and research-based insights led to a learning opportunity for everyone in attendance. A.J. has worked at all levels of the K–12 spectrum and has the lens of a parent as well. He will encourage educators to not only be intentional about innovation, but also to focus on how our practice needs to always be centered on the student experience.

WHAT PEOPLE ARE SAYING ABOUT A.J. JULIANI

"I was captivated by your presentation. Honestly, most keynote addresses usually don't hit home, but yours definitely got my brain working overtime."

"The best keynote I've been to in a long time. Thank you for sharing with us. I hope to be mindful of this inspirational feeling always."

"I really can't explain how awesome A.J. Juliani is! Inspiring, funny and more importantly, making me reflect on my practice."

POPULAR MESSAGES FROM A.J. JULIANI

Many of A.J.'s presentations are created specifically for your event, audience, and school. To get a sense of the topics A.J. presents on most, here are some keynote presentations he has done in the past:

1. Empower: What Happens When Students Own Their Learning

2. The Power of Inquiry and Choice: 20% Time and Genius Hour Projects

3. Intentional Innovation: How to Guide Risk-Taking, Build Creative Capacity, and Lead Change

4. Student-Centered Classrooms for Today's Student: Engaging All Learners Through Choice, Technology, and Innovative Practices

5. Technology with a Purpose: Empowering Students with Choice and Technology

6. Design Thinking and the Maker Movement in K–12

CONNECT

Connect with A.J. Juliani for more information about bringing him to your event.

Email: ajjuliani@gmail.com

Twitter: @ajjuliani

Blog: ajjuliani.com

Made in the USA
San Bernardino, CA
01 March 2019